The Big Shot

TOMMY GEMMELL

The Big Shot

 STANLEY PAUL: *London*

STANLEY PAUL & CO LTD
178–202 Great Portland Street, London W1

AN IMPRINT OF THE HUTCHINSON GROUP

London Melbourne Sydney
Auckland Bombay Toronto
Johannesburg New York

★

First published 1968
Reprinted October 1968

This book has been set in Times, and printed in
Great Britain on Antique Wove paper by
The Camelot Press Ltd., London and Southampton
and bound by Wm. Brendon, Tiptree, Essex

09 089240 2

Contents

Illustrations

Foreword

By manager Jock Stein, Celtic F.C.

THERE is a great deal I could say about Tommy Gemmell, but I think the highest tribute to him has already been paid by many of our opponents.

Through the years it has been accepted in football that a full-back's job was to mark the winger. Yet for some time it has been obvious that teams playing against us have instructed their wingers to mark Tommy!

They realize that although he takes the field as a defender he is always ready to move into the attack and so they cannot afford to overlook him. As I see it he has brought a new excitement into full-back play because there is nothing more spectacular than the sight of a player charging down the field time and again and letting fly with a full-blooded shot when he gets the chance.

It means a lot of hard running for Tommy. Yet he is always willing to do it. And I want to point out that he developed this technique himself by sheer hard work and so he fully deserves the success which has come his way.

Tommy, of course, is a bit of a showman, and a lot of what he does is 'off the cuff'. Having said that, I can assure you his style of play is still very much a part of our pattern. Our method at Parkhead is to have a general pattern which will leave scope for one or two unorthodox players.

A player like Gemmell is important to a team because his spectacular shooting provides the supporters with the kind of entertainment they want. It has also brought us some valuable goals and I'm sure everyone who reads this book will enjoy his description of the equalizer he scored in the European Cup Final in Lisbon. None of us who saw that goal are ever likely to forget it.

It seems to me that in this book Tommy has done exactly
what he does on the field in every game . . . he has covered a
lot of ground!

I know you will agree with me that football needs person-
alities. Tommy Gemmell is one of them. People see him as a
'Gay Cavalier' on the field and I think you will find this side
of his personality coming through in the pages that follow.

Introduction

I HESITATED when the idea of writing a book was first put to me. It seemed then that at twenty-four I was a bit too young to write about my career. I thought maybe I should wait a few years and see what else happened to me.

Now I'm glad I decided not to wait. Because when I really got down to thinking about the terrific experiences I've had as a Celtic player, and with Scotland too, I found that the events of the last few years were still vivid in my mind. They came back to me so clearly that every detail was there and I could remember my feelings at the time. But I think if I had waited a few years, even an unforgettable event like the European Cup Final would have been less clear in my mind.

I've enjoyed looking back on the success I have been lucky to share with Celtic and I hope readers will get some pleasure out of it too. Speaking of readers, I realize you may not all agree with my assessment of famous players in the pages that follow, but I hope you will accept that these are honest opinions formed from my personal experience of these players.

I am well aware, of course, that if it was not for the efforts of a number of other people I should not be writing this book at all. So I should first like to thank all my mates at Parkhead for providing this chance. I should have precious little to write about now if they had not achieved so much as a team.

I also want to thank manager Jock Stein. Not only for his kind remarks in the Foreword, but for all his help on and off the field since he came to Parkhead. There is a great deal more I have to say about him, but I've kept it for other chapters.

Finally, I must mention Glasgow journalist Ian Peebles, who helped me get my ideas and memories down on paper.

A South American Liberty!

EVER since 1960 the European champions have met the top team in South America for a Trophy called the Inter-Continental Cup. That name is hardly ever used, however, as everyone accepts that this home-and-home fixture is for the World Championship—the supreme status symbol in club football. So I imagine there are lots of youngsters in many countries who dream of playing in these very special show games.

Frankly, my advice to all of them is . . . FORGET IT! Aim as high as you like in football but don't worry if you never get to play for that World title because then your dream might just become a nightmare—and as a Celtic player I can speak from bitter experience. We were the first British club ever to play for the Inter-Continental Cup and naturally it was a terrific honour. It was a great feeling too to be going forward as Europe's champions, knowing that only one team stood between you and the World title.

In 1967 we thought we could win that title. We were playing good football and we were a better side than the South Americans. But that was before we knew very much about our opponents, Racing Club of Argentina. Later, we were to discover that their plans for winning the World Crown had very little to do with football.

These Argentinians were like no team I had ever encountered before. Indeed, I think it is fair to say that they were the dirtiest, most ruthless, and despicable bunch of soccer hatchet-men ever gathered together under the one set of jerseys. In all grades of football you'll find the tough guy and the 'fly' man, but Racing Club were in a class of their own.

They were the masters at heel-clicking and catching you

with their elbow when the ball was well away and they had
long since perfected every other dirty trick known in football,
including a fair amount of spitting. I'm not saying they took
us by surprise. The Boss, Jock Stein, had compiled a pretty
thick dossier on them before they reached Scotland and he
warned us that in the first leg at Hampden they would try to
slow the game down. We knew then there would be a certain
amount of trouble, as the best way to slow any game down is
to commit as many fouls as possible. We were just as determined not to let them knock us out of our stride.

The Hampden tie worked out as anticipated. They played
a purely destructive game and we refused to be upset. Self-
discipline was easy for us on that October evening because as
far as behaviour was concerned this game was no different
from any other. Every player at Parkhead knows he will get
no sympathy if he is guilty of field offences. In fact, although
it was well into the second half before Billy McNeill headed
the winner I think we all gained confidence from this match
because Racing did not appear to have very much to offer in
the finer points of football, although they gave us one or two
hints that they knew a thing or two about unarmed combat.

It was not until the second leg in Buenos Aires, however,
that we fully realized why Racing are known as the 'dirtiest
team in South America'. The astonishing thing is that their
coach, Jose Pizzuti, is a most pleasant wee man off duty and
was a really skilful player in his day. You would think he
would seek the same kind of reputation for his team. Instead,
when he went for that coaching certificate, he must have
studied under SMERSH!

Ten days after the Hampden game we were flying in over
the skyscrapers of Buenos Aires to prepare for the second leg.
At that time we were an optimistic outfit because we sensed that
the Boss believed we were capable of getting the draw which
would be enough to give us the World title. We moved out
immediately to the luxurious Hindu Club and on that first
Sunday we got off to a light-hearted start.

As it was a day of Obligation most of our party went off to find the nearest Catholic church. That left the Boss, Bertie Auld, Willie Wallace, Ronnie Simpson and myself. So we headed for the golf course. And what a start the Boss made. Over the first nine holes he played as if he had been searching for that course all his life. His drives went off like rockets and his irons were bang on line. No wonder all the wee local boys skipped around his heels and fought to pull his clubs. They knew class when they saw it and the Boss looked at us as if we were lucky to be playing with him. He was in a great mood and, like any golfer who thinks he has suddenly found the secret, he could hardly keep the smile off his face.

Then the bubble burst. After the turn the Boss's ball began to go in all directions and the wee boys retreated to a safe distance. Even the smallest member of the gallery soon realized that old man Simpson, commonly known as 'faither', was the real golfer in the company. By the eighteenth he had the gallery to himself and the Boss was pulling his own caddie-car.

Yet I think I remember that round of golf because it was the only time during our stay in South America that I saw him looking really relaxed. Usually he hides his feelings well, especially in the tension before a big game, but he was obviously concerned about these matches with Racing Club.

The strain the Boss was under would show through during training sessions. Usually, as we train, a lot of cross-talk goes on and the Boss is liable to take as much a part in it as anybody, but in those days before the tie in Buenos Aires he would turn on anyone who was capering about and tell them: 'That's enough. We're here to work' . . . or words to that effect. So we were all on our best behaviour while we stayed at the Hindu Club. Even if we thought we were good enough to get the draw which would give us the title, we sensed it was going to be no picnic.

And when we reached the Avellanda Stadium our worst

fears were justified. Even before the game started, as we loosened up and hit a few shots at goal, Ronnie Simpson suddenly staggered and put his hands to his head. He had been hit. A narrow rectangular piece of iron, about two inches long, had been thrown through the fence which is supposed to protect the players.

Boy, were we angry! It was ridiculous that a thing like that should happen to any player before such a game. Ronnie, dazed, shocked, and obviously in pain couldn't possibly play and it meant that our reserve John Fallon suddenly found himself playing in a World tie at two minutes' notice. At least he hardly had time to get nervous, but I could not help thinking this was one time when fate wasn't working for Celtic.

Yet despite Ronnie's injury and despite all the unfriendly Argentinians in that stadium, we actually came very near to victory in Buenos Aires. In fact, we scored first. With what was virtually his last gesture of neutrality, the referee awarded us a penalty. I never took a kick with more determination and it was worth a guinea a box to see the expression on the faces of Racing Club. The turning-point came, however, when Jimmy Johnstone scored what looked like a perfectly good second goal, only to have it chalked off. Racing equalized after that, yet at the interval we still thought we had a chance. The Boss urged us, as he had done before the kick-off, not to 'annoy' either Racing or their supporters. He couldn't have guessed how difficult this was going to be!

For Racing got their second goal soon after the interval and from there on they decided to take no chances. Their tackling became worse and worse and after a while you didn't need to decide whether to pass or hold the ball, because if you did not get rid of it immediately, somebody was sure to send you sprawling. Jimmy Johnstone suffered more than most of us, but we all had to remember, firstly, not to annoy the Argentinians.

Well, we didn't annoy them. Instead they hacked, tripped,

and pushed their way to a 2–1 victory which earned them a third-game play-off for the title which they were obviously determined to get at all costs. We trooped back to our dressing-room, disgusted. I'll never forget it. We were so incensed at the treatment we had had to take from these South American soccer gangsters. Nobody made a dive for the bath as they would normally do. We just sat there trying to think of words bad enough to describe Racing Club who had obviously been confident the Uruguayan referee would let them away with anything.

Then we were joined in the dressing-room by our own officials. Chairman Bob Kelly told us he would not allow us to play a third game against these opponents. I think that cheered most of us up because we were so fed up with the whole affair we would have liked nothing better than to grab the first plane back to Glasgow.

Half an hour later we would have been happy to settle for a 'pass-out' from that dressing-room. The atmosphere had become chaotic. Argentinian and Uruguayan officials poured in when they heard we did not want to play the third game in Montevideo, and they were followed by Press men, photographers, police, and anyone in Buenos Aires who had nothing better to do at the time. At least, that's how it seemed because there was simply no room to move and most of us had still not changed.

As the flash-bulbs went off and interpreters tried to sort out the various arguments, it was difficult to know whether our next destination would be Scotland or Uruguay. At one stage the Boss asked us if we were prepared to play Racing Club again and we said 'Yes', mainly because we could tell from his attitude that he thought we could still win the third game if we got protection from the referee. The Uruguayans assured us the next game would be strictly controlled, and finally Mr. Kelly took their word for it.

I didn't know then, of course, that if the Chairman had been adamant and refused to play in Montevideo I would

have been spared the most embarrassing football experience
of my career . . . but I'll tell you about that later.

We had cheered up a lot by the time we flew out to Uruguay the next day. We had heard that the fans in Montevideo
didn't like Racing Club at all and were sure to be behind us.
And any doubts we may have had about this story were
quickly dispelled at the airport. We got a great reception, the
crowds were shouting 'Celtic, Celtic' and that really gave our
morale a boost. It pleased us even more when we were visited
at our hotel by the Penarol players, the former World
Champions who had played us in a friendly at Parkhead.
They confirmed that Racing Club had a reputation for being
a really nasty bunch, but they were sure we could still beat
them.

The Boss must have been cheered by all this too because
there were two occasions when he showed how quick he can
be with the gags. There was a phone call and one of the
waiters in the hotel came up to him and asked: 'Are you
Stein?' In the local accent, however, it sounded like 'Are you
stayin'?'—and quick as a flash the Big Man replied: 'No, I'm
leaving on Sunday.'

Outside the hotel the following day he really had us rolling
about. We had been invited to go to a nearby shop where we
could get some bargains in clothes. The proprietor was
delighted to see us. He wore a broad smile and, like me, he
had the kind of nose which leaves very little room for the rest
of your face. 'This is wonderful,' he said. 'To think you come
all the way from Glasgow to my shop. And you know what?
I've got a cousin in Glasgow. Maybe you know him. His
name's Levy.'

The rest of us smilingly shook our heads. Our clothier
friend obviously didn't realize how many people there are
around Glasgow with a name like Levy. But the Boss had the
answer. After a moment he said: 'Levy? Sure I know him.
Your cousin must be Betting Levy!'

As the rest of us nearly choked trying not to laugh, the

Montevideo man could hardly contain himself. 'Sure, sure,' he cried, 'that sounds like him. But is he doing well?'

Back came the deadpan reply: 'Doing well? He takes in a fortune every week!'

That was the news this leading light in Montevideo Menswear had been waiting for. He could hardly serve us after that because he was obviously bursting to spread the word among his relations that their nearly-forgotten cousin in Scotland was making a fortune and seemed to be a household name.

This little bit of kidding by the Boss gave the clothier a great deal of pleasure—and it helped the Celtic camp a lot too. It gave us something to look back and laugh about for the rest of the day and as the 'decider' approached our mood of optimism was increasing. Yet at the same time our preparations were deadly serious—so serious that Bertie Auld and I were nearly thrown out of the team altogether!

It happened like this. On the afternoon before the game Bertie and I sat in the hotel lounge chatting to some Press men. Time passed quickly and it was a long while before we realized we were the only players around. No wonder. Up in one of the rooms the Boss was holding his final tactics talk and nobody had noticed we were missing. By the time we sheepishly put our heads round the door the meeting was almost over. Later the Boss had a few things to say to both of us and he finished by telling us very frankly that if the next day's game had been anything less important than a World tie we would have been out of the team and in the grandstand.

Since we were in we were able to join the rest of the boys in a search for a huge Uruguayan flag. It had been decided that since the local fans were supposed to be on our side they would back us even more if we went out with their flag. So about twenty minutes before the kick-off we all strolled on to the field, waved, acted like a most friendly bunch of fellas, then unfurled the flag. The fans seemed to like the gesture, but their response wasn't quite as enthusiastic as we had

hoped. Back in the pavilion we soon found the answer.
Someone told us that ten minutes earlier the Racing Club
party had been out waving an even bigger Uruguayan flag
than ours!

Yes, one up for the Argentinians—and a lesson to us all
that no matter how smart you may think you are in these top
international competitions you should always remember that
the other fellow is thinking too and he may come up with an
even better idea than you. It's this kind of thing, no doubt,
which puts an extra strain on managers.

Before the game the Boss warned us, as usual, of the need
for self-control. He no doubt hoped, as we all did, that the
assurances given about firm refereeing would keep the wild
men of Racing Club in check. Yet I'm sure he sensed by our
mood that if the South Americans kicked, hacked, and spat
at us any more we would do a wee bit of Scottish 'sorting out'.

It was obvious, after hardly any time at all, that Racing had
no intention of altering their tactics. Our appeals to the
referee were a pure waste of time and after one particularly
vicious foul on Jimmy Johnstone I think we all decided that
was the last straw. I could see our blokes were no longer
holding back and the game became nothing more than an
outdoor exhibition of unarmed combat.

The Paraguayan referee was not slow, however, to spot
crimes committed by anybody in a Celtic jersey and as the
game went on John Hughes, Jimmy Johnstone, and Bobby
Lennox were all ordered off and Racing had the one-goal
lead which they no doubt felt justified all their diabolical
tactics.

So, as near as I can guess, there would be about ten minutes
to go when I decided that justice had to be done. After the
umpteenth incident players and officials were gathered round
the referee and Bertie Auld. It was all very heated and everyone was trying to see what was happening . . . but one player
was standing apart. He was making sure he wouldn't be
involved. I wasn't surprised because he had managed to stay

out of all the real trouble throughout the tie. This was Raffo, wearing a No. 11 jersey and looking quite pleased with himself. It made me so annoyed to think that the tie was nearly over and this man looked like finishing it unscathed, yet of all the members of the ruthless Racing team he had been the most consistently dirty. Yet he was crafty enough to do all his spitting and kicking when the referee was looking the other way. Nobody had been able to get their own back on him because he jumped high in the air every time you tried to tackle him. As I looked at him I thought: 'I bet he's thinking the Scots are a soft lot because he's "given us stick" all that time and got away with it.' All this had gone through my mind in a matter of seconds and in sheer temper I decided to hand out justice myself. I ran quickly round to where he was standing and kicked him. The swing was well timed, the aim was good too, and my boot landed on a very tender spot. Mr. Raffo squealed like a pig and went down in a heap. I quickly returned to my previous stance feeling very, very pleased with myself. Because of the fuss round Bertie hardly anyone had seen my little deed and it did my heart good to know that Raffo had got what was coming to him.

Now, I'm not going to defend myself. I'm not suggesting this was a nice thing to do. If another player annoys you it is no solution to kick him deliberately. But in this instance it seemed the only way to deal with him. Racing Club had set their own standards in these matches and to get down to them you had to stoop pretty low.

Mark you, I had no idea what an infamous kick that was to become. I certainly never dreamed I would have to spend days, even weeks, explaining it when I got back to Glasgow.

The trouble began when, on the Wednesday evening after we returned home from South America, the B.B.C. showed a film taken during the game in Montevideo. I never saw it so I was completely taken by surprise when I arrived at Parkhead on the following morning and the first few people I met said: 'You're some guy you. . . . What a daft thing to do in front of the cameras! . . . What a fool you are!' And I couldn't even start to print some of the other things which were said to me in the days that followed.

It seemed that the B.B.C. had managed to get hold of a film which highlighted most of the fouls committed by Celtic and somehow missed the dirty work done by the Argentinians. And I was assured that by far the most dramatic shots were of a bloke called Gemmell kicking a bloke who was standing minding his own business.

Yes, while I had been getting my revenge on Raffo a TV camera high in the stands had followed my every move. I haven't seen that particular film yet, but I've been told often enough that my hasty retreat after delivering the blow did not look particularly dignified on the screen. I thought I was just helping the cause of justice . . . but I never thought justice would be seen to be done by about ten million British viewers, including my family and friends. I was widely criticized, of course, especially by English critics who had been waiting for an opportunity to knock Celtic. They had been shocked when we won the European Cup; annoyed that we had done so much more than any of their teams.

Even my mother said to me the first time I visited her after the TV film had been shown: 'Why did you have to go and kick that man?' I explained, as I've tried to explain here, and I think she understood. Many other people still think what I did to Raffo was outrageous, but I think they will understand the atmosphere in Montevideo better when I tell this story, which has never been told before.

The fact is, the most amazing thing about that game, as far as I was concerned, happened as I was walking off the field, Raffo ran over to me . . . and he was smiling. He made signals and at first I thought he was looking for a fight! Then I realized he wanted to swap jerseys with me. Swapping jerseys is an international football custom, of course, but you tend to do more of it in a game where relations have been good. It seemed strange to me in that situation and I admit I was suspicious. I thought: 'This bloke probably wants me to pull the jersey over my head so he can belt me one when I can't see him.'

But Raffo looked so darned friendly I felt I could hardly turn him down. So I warily got out of one sleeve first, then the other, then, stepping back quickly, I whipped my jersey over my head. His smile became even broader, and as we swapped jerseys he warmly shook my hand. Indeed, as he ran towards the tunnel he had a grin on his face and, in English, he shouted a little remark about the accuracy of my kick.

In the game of football as we know it, it seems unlikely that Raffo should have anything to do with me. But at home, among my other souvenirs, I have a neatly pressed Racing Club jersey with vertical blue and white stripes and a No. 11 on the back which proves that its former owner was less upset by that kick than the millions of TV fans who saw it in Britain.

Players like him kick—and expect to be kicked. It is the way some of them play the game. Referees in most European countries would not stand for such behaviour. That's why I started off this chapter by warning youngsters that playing in the World Club Championship is an experience they can probably do well without. I feel certain Celtic would not take part again in similar circumstances. It is a good idea that the European Champions should meet the Champions of South America each year, but these games are going to get out of control too often unless there is a neutral venue.

I would play the World final in New York. It might deprive the clubs of a financial bonanza, but if the referee was a thoroughly reliable man, carefully selected, then we could be sure the winners would be worthy champions. I certainly think no British team should ever agree to a World series in which two of the three matches could be played in South America. If the 1967 title had been decided over ninety minutes in a neutral country there is no doubt we would have been able to take it back to Parkhead.

As it was, our encounter with Racing Club brought us nothing but trouble. After we got home, and even after the TV film, another shock awaited those of us who had played in Montevideo.

One morning during training we were told the Chairman wanted to meet us at 11.30. The Boss admitted that it had to do with our behaviour in that third game in Uruguay. Celtic through the years had always had a good reputation for discipline on the field and it had certainly been tarnished in Montevideo. There had to be a punishment and the Boss wanted our opinion on whether it should be spread over the entire team or merely those who had been sent off. We immediately said it should be a team affair. He had known what our answer would be anyway.

So there were eleven very shocked individuals in Parkhead that morning when Mr. Kelly announced that the Board had decided to fine each of us £250!

There were those who thought this was just a gesture to impress the public and that we would never really have to pay all that money. But they didn't know Bob Kelly. He doesn't do things like that—and every penny of the fine was deducted from bonuses which we had earned previously in other matches.

Mr. Kelly was also ready, however, to accept part of the responsibility. As he announced the fines he confessed that he should have stuck to his original decision in Buenos Aires. He said he ought never to have allowed us to play in that third game and that he had no doubt in his own mind that he had made a mistake.

I think everyone would agree with him now. If we had refused to play the third game, especially after what happened to Ronnie Simpson, football people everywhere would have been on our side. Many would have regarded us as the best team in the world even if we had no official title. But it is easy to be wise after the event.

2

This was the Game

I THINK the most difficult question a footballer can be asked is: 'What was the greatest game you played in?'

The answer, after all, doesn't depend so much on the player's memory as on what the person who asks the question really means. He may be thinking of the game which affected the player's career most or where he played better than any other. He may mean the most exciting game or the one with the most colourful background.

If a player has been lucky enough, as I have, to be in a team which has had a lot of success in recent years then there are plenty of matches to choose from. That first Cup Final is one you will always remember and the international where you got your first 'cap' because it meant a lot to the family. These were important moments in your career, yet they might not have been 'great games'. You may have played badly in them. As we all know the greatest matches are not always at Hampden or Wembley anyway. It can happen that twenty-two players excel themselves on a muddy pitch in an unglamorous ground during a League match.

But when people ask me about 'the greatest game' I presume they mean the one I will remember when I've forgotten about most of the others. I think of the game which meant most to me. I remember the tremendous feeling of satisfaction and pride when the final whistle went. I've no doubts at all about what was the greatest game I ever took part in.

Yes, and I'll bet you think I'm going to talk about Celtic's European Cup Final win in Lisbon! Well, I'm coming to that quite soon, but it's not the game I am thinking about right now.

There was no bright sun for the game which is uppermost

in my mind—and it wasn't played in a super stadium. In fact, the Juliska Stadium is a pretty ordinary unattractive ground with little cover for spectators and no special atmosphere to inspire players. It is the home of the famous Czech Army team Dukla and is in Prague. The Czech capital can be a grim sort of city at any time, but when we visited it last year it was bitterly cold and on the day of the match there was a dampness in the air too.

The weather didn't bother us, of course. In our mood then nothing could have depressed us because we were in Prague to play Dukla in the second leg of the European Cup—and we had a 3-1 lead after meeting them at Parkhead.

We also had a special plan. We were going to play defensively for the entire game, which was in complete contrast to our usual style. In our talks about the match we had decided that Dukla, judging by the way they played at Parkhead, didn't have the pace to upset us if we played it tight. We didn't think they had the stamina to attack throughout a game either, as they had too many veteran players in the side.

Yet we knew the Prague match would be no cakewalk. Dukla had a lot more experience of European football than we had and in these ties a two-goal lead can disappear in the time it takes to make a couple of silly mistakes. But we were determined there would be no mistakes that day. We knew that provided the Czechs scored no more than one goal then we should be through to the final of the European Cup.

In that first half Dukla had their chances . . . and missed them. Any team allowed to attack is bound to get chances, but players tend to make a hurried attempt in these circumstances because they know that in a packed defence they are sure to be challenged quickly. At half-time there was no scoring and I admit I was getting pretty excited in the second half as I realized every minute was taking us nearer the final and Dukla were getting a Czechoslovakian 'raspberry' from their own supporters. We didn't try to be clever. We just kept sending long balls up to Stevie Chalmers who, even as a

Tommy Gemmell, Celtic

Opposite, above: That's me on the left of the front row with my school team. I was eleven then. Why twelve players? I don't know, I was too busy squeezing into the picture

Opposite, below: My junior team, Coltness United, in season 1961–2. I'm second from the left in the back row

This page, above: We were in Rothesay for a Boys' Brigade camp. I was fourteen then and beginning to get a bit of height

This page, below: My wife Anne and I doing a 'happy couple' pose

A handshake from Princess Alexandra. A bow from me

It's Rangers first goal at Parkhead in the vital New Year game last season. John Fallon, on his knees, hammers the ground. Orjan Persson waves. And I'm in the middle, speechless

one-man forward line, managed to give the Dukla defenders something to think about.

Fifteen minutes left to go and still no scoring. . . . Then just ten minutes. . . . I could tell by the signs from our boys at the side of the field—and by their faces—that we were nearly there. In the last few minutes I could hardly concentrate on the game as I realized we were really going to do it.

Then at last, with the score still 0–0, I heard the final whistle! I wanted to jump through the clouds. I wanted to hug everybody on the field. I couldn't stop laughing, yet the lump in my throat had me near to crying. For it was such a great moment for Celtic. We had just become the first British side to reach the European Cup Final. Few people had thought we could do it, because it was supposed to be near to impossible. Manchester United, Spurs, and Liverpool at their best, Hibs, Dundee, and Rangers had all reached the semifinals, but none had broken the barrier which led to the final. English writers who had looked down their noses at Scottish football for years had still said, even after we beat Dukla at Parkhead, that we would fail in Prague. Maybe they hoped we would fail because otherwise there could never be the same glory in the European Cup for an English team.

On that cold afternoon in the Juliska Stadium I knew, we all knew, that we had made the big breakthrough. No matter what any other British team might do in the years to come we would always be remembered as the first to reach the final. We had put Celtic's name in the history books. It may seem difficult to understand now, but at that moment none of us gave a thought to winning the Cup. That just didn't matter. We had reached our target. I remembered how from early in the season when we knew we were going well, 'Luggy' Clark and I, who drove in to Parkhead from Motherwell every morning in those days, used to talk about our chances. We'd imagine what it would be like; what people would say, if we won everything. Then we would agree that it would be marvellous if we not only won one of the top prizes in Scotland, but also managed to reach the final of the European Cup. For we knew this was the thing nobody believed we could do.

You will understand now, I think, why that game in Prague will always stick in my mind. The quality of the football was nothing special. What mattered was the tremendous feeling of achievement after the result.

And, you know, I think I'll remember the celebrations after that game almost as much as the tie itself. The champagne was out in the dressing-room, of course, but that was only the beginning because we had arranged to fly home immediately after the game. And what a flight that was! The airline must have known we were going to reach the final because they had a big cake ready when we got on the plane. They also had champagne ready for us . . . bottles and bottles of the stuff. The supplies never ran out and the air hostesses were wonderful too, joining in the spirit of the party. The flight lasted around three hours, but with the amount of bubbles popping around the plane I'm sure it could have stayed airborne for a fortnight without fuel.

None of us make a habit of drinking a great deal as a rule, but I thought the story of that party was important because it showed how overjoyed everyone attached to Celtic— players and officials—were at reaching the European Final. Our supporters showed how they felt too when they gave us a great welcome at the airport that night.

I couldn't write a book like this without giving some space to the European Cup Final against Milan in Lisbon. There I scored what was possibly the most important goal of my career. That apart, it was an unforgettable game for us all. Yet our feelings towards it were so different from when we were in Prague. I think we were more relaxed in Lisbon than at any time during the season . . . and no doubt that was why we played so well.

Weeks before we met Inter-Milan in the final, however, things seemed to be going our way. While we got smartly through by drawing in Prague, it took Milan three games with Sofia of Bulgaria before they finally booked their place in the final. The Italians weren't convincing against Sofia and while we finished the season by winning everything at home, then got down to a thorough preparation for Lisbon, our opponents were still playing League fixtures in their own country and failing to get impressive results. The reports then were that Inter were a tired team, but we didn't care what state they were in.

As we trained and planned at Seamill we became more and more optimistic about beating them. We had hoped all along that if we met them it would be in the final because then they couldn't stay in their defensive shell. In a final you must attack at some time if you are to win. The Boss had studied their tactics and we knew just what to expect from them. For our part we had planned everything to the last detail and everybody knew exactly what he had to do.

I think we became really confident, nevertheless, after something the Boss said near the end of our stay at Seamill. He does not believe in predictions and will talk about everything except the actual result as we prepare for a game, but after one of our discussions he suddenly said: 'If we play properly, the way we can play, then we'll win the European Cup.'

He was really telling us we would have to hit our best form, but we reckoned he must feel pretty confident when he was ready to commit himself as far as that. It was nice to know he felt that way and so when we flew to Portugal and moved into our hotel in Estoril a few days before the final we hadn't a care in the world.

As fate would have it I was sharing a room, for the first time on any trip, with fellow full-back Jim Craig. That was quite a coincidence because in the years to come, no matter when I look back on the Lisbon game, I will always remember the part played by this character Craig, who is better known at Parkhead by his nickname 'Cairney'. As you may have guessed, he got the name because Scottish actor John

Cairney played the title part in the TV series *This Man Craig*.

Right now, I think, is a good time to say something about 'This Man Craig' as a player. I have the feeling, for instance, that he is very close to being a great full-back. His big trouble, of course, is that he is so casual . . . or at any rate, he looks casual. No matter how much pressure you are under, Jim takes the ball and moves it around as if there wasn't another player within a hundred yards of him. Time and again I've held my breath as he calmly dribbled out of a tight spot where we could all have been in trouble if he had lost possession. Frankly, Jim never appears to be in a hurry and he has a running style which makes him look relaxed even when he is covering the ground pretty quickly.

Off the field he is a quiet type who takes a bit of getting to know—and I don't mind telling you there was one time when I wished I had known him less!

He was working at the Dental Hospital in Glasgow as part of his course to become a dentist and during training one day he had let us know that if we needed treatment all we had to do was look him up. As I had been having a bit of trouble for a while with a tooth I decided to give him my custom.

'Cairney' couldn't get me in the chair quick enough and I didn't complain, because he had two attractive young girl students assisting him. He looked at the tooth and they had a look too, then he said it would need filling. They smiled a bit at the time, but I never thought much about it.

I had plenty to think about straight afterwards when 'Cairney' told me: 'I think you would be better with an injection before this filling.' So he gave me a big one, but after it somehow I could still feel everything. So he gave me a second. Then, when it seemed as if he must have penetrated far into the Gemmell interior, a surgeon came along. He looked at the tooth; then at my torturer; then said: 'I'm sorry, Mr. Craig, but in this case the tooth is better out.'

By that time I had gone off our man Craig and I said: 'You're some bloke you, why didn't you just take it out in the first place?' He looked glum, but didn't answer. And as soon as he touched my tooth with the pliers I jumped. The effect of the 'jabs' had worn off and I needed two more because the tooth was a stubborn one. In fact, during the struggle the metal handles of the pliers snapped on Jim's finger and split it. With blood gushing out 'Cairney' went off for a dressing and his two assistants were highly amused. I asked them to let me in on the joke and they explained how he and I had both suffered because he had tried to be clever. The only reason he hadn't taken the tooth out in the first place was because more marks are awarded in the hospital for a filling than for an extraction!

What with four injections and a split finger my dental appointment with 'Cairney' was a painful experience for both of us. In Estoril, however, we enjoyed ourselves thoroughly and I got to know Jim a lot better . . . yet I never knew quite what to expect from him.

I was getting ready for bed, for instance, on the night before the final when he suddenly said: 'You know, I think I'm going to be brilliant tomorrow.' It was a remark completely out of character because Jim isn't one of those big-heads who like to tell you how good they are. I laughed at first because I thought he was joking, but then I realized he was deadly serious.

Maybe it still sounds like a big-headed remark to other people, but I know Jim never intended it that way. I think, like the rest of us, he had become a lot more professional in that season. He had obviously been thinking about the tactics we planned to use against Inter and had realized that they suited him down to the ground and so he was bound to play well. In fact, his prophecy was dead right. He *was* brilliant . . . especially in the second half. But wait, I'll come back to that part.

What I remember most about Estoril on the day of the game was how relaxed we were—and how worried everyone else seemed to be! In the late afternoon, for instance, trainer

Neil Mochan said he wanted us out on the lawn beside our
hotel for some loosening-up exercises. At first we pretended
we were not going out as we didn't need to loosen up to beat
Inter-Milan, but when we did go out there were quite a few
supporters gathered round the lawn. And I've never seen
such a nervous bunch. I went over to a bookmaker friend who
was there with his wife and she was really keyed up. 'Do you
think it's going to be all right, Tommy?' she kept asking.
'Will you beat them?' In fact, everyone around seemed to be
asking: 'Will it be all right?' Our supporters had planned for
the Lisbon game for so long and travelled so far they could
hardly bear to think of the anti-climax it would be if we lost. I
think perhaps that training session did the spectators more
good than it did us because they were able to see we were
relaxed and confident. Two other people I had to reassure
that afternoon were Motherwell car dealer Ian Skelly and his
father. I told them there was 'no danger' and as I left them
Mr. Skelly, Senior, gripped my arm and said: 'If you score
today you can have thirty gallons of petrol when you get
home.'

Actually, I think I could write a whole book about the
small things which happened before and during the European
Cup Final because I've relived that day so often.

Yet there is no doubt that the most amazing thing about
our performance—about everything we did—was this confidence which we all shared. I didn't think about it at the
time, but looking back now I can see that it must have
astonished everyone we encountered . . . especially Inter-
Milan. By top international standards we were just a bunch
of youngsters, virtually unknown as individuals outside of
Scotland. We were about to play the most famous club in the
world at that time, Internazionale of Milan. They were a
tremendously experienced side, full of high-priced individuals.
They had won the European and World crowns in 1964 and
1965. They were recognized as the greatest defensive side
ever seen in Europe.

Yet we expected to beat them! Why? I'm sure it was because we had no fear of losing to them. It didn't matter if we lost because we had already achieved everything. We had realized our greatest ambition by becoming the first British team to reach the European Cup Final and we had won every honour in Scotland. We had nothing to lose that sunny evening in Lisbon.

Even as we lined up outside the dressing-rooms before going out to the field the Italians must have noticed we were a cheery bunch. They were absolutely baffled, however, by what happened next. There is a walk of about two hundred yards from the dressing-rooms to the pitch at the National Stadium in Lisbon. You go along a tree-lined path and then through a tunnel and it was here that Bertie Auld gave us the final psychological advantage. As the teams marched along together he started singing the 'Celtic Song' and we all joined in. You could tell from the expression on the Milan men's faces that they thought they had run against a bunch of Scottish madmen. At that moment they must also have realized we were not a bit afraid of them.

We made them well aware of that on the field too, although we could hardly have got off to a worse start. After only eight minutes we were a goal down when Mazzola scored with a penalty kick. In that first spell I was conscious of the heat, and my legs felt heavy, but after about twenty minutes I got my second wind and I felt terrific. We were doing all the attacking and although Sarti was brilliant in the Milan goal I felt sure we were bound to score.

At half-time we were still behind, but the Boss told us to stick to exactly the same technique, although he warned those who were crossing the ball to pull it back to the edge of the penalty box as the Italians were getting everything in their goal area.

After the interval we really sailed into them. Everyone was going forward and Jim Craig was coming into his own.

Playing with terrific confidence he was striding down the

right wing as if Inter didn't exist. Three times after the interval he moved deep into Milan territory and sent over crosses which gave Sarti and his chums plenty to think about. Then in the sixty-third minute (although I didn't know the time then!) Craig went off again with a pass from Bobby Murdoch who was in midfield. After Bobby parted with the ball he ran away towards the inside-left position, taking a man with him. This left a wide gap in the centre of the field and I started to run.

Jim, looking as casual as ever, was still heading towards the corner flag. It seemed as if he was about to put over another cross I started to shout 'Cairney, Cairney'. I knew if he cut the ball back I would be in a great position for a shot and as I came near to their penalty area I was still shouting.

Then, at exactly the right moment, he stroked the ball across to me. It was a great pass, coming at just the right speed, and asking to be hit. An Italian, who might have blocked my shot, shirked the tackle when he saw me running in at full tilt and I hit the ball first time with my right. It felt good . . . and when I lifted my head it looked good. The ball was flying into the net. I had scored. We were level and still had almost half an hour to play. No wonder 'Cairney' had a huge smile on his face.

That was the most important goal I've ever scored and the one most people will remember, because it knocked the heart out of Inter. They must have known, as we did, that it was only a matter of time before we would score again. Sure enough, Stevie Chalmers got the winner six minutes from time. Later that night when I was telling 'Cairney' for the umpteenth time what a great pass it had been, he said: 'Ach, I knew you were coming through all the time, I just waited until you were in the right place.'

Finally, on the subject of Lisbon, I should tell you that my friend Mr. Skelly didn't forget his offer. Weeks after the final I went into one of his stations and was told: 'There's thirty gallons of petrol waiting here for you.' So you could say that goal against Inter took me quite a long way!

3

Two Hours with Mr. Kelly

BY the end of season 1966-7, when Celtic had won the European Cup, the Scottish League Championship, the Scottish Cup, the League Cup, and the Glasgow Cup—every competition we entered—even the English sports writers were admitting we were a pretty good team. Although it must have broken their hearts to have to praise a Scottish side, our record-breaking run forced them to concede that our teamwork was terrific, although they clearly didn't think too much of us individually.

Actually these blokes never got near to the truth. They never realized Celtic achieved what they did because they were a great club . . . and still are. Football is more than just a team affair, after all, and when you go so far as to become European champions the entire club must be sound.

We had good players who worked well together. We were also lucky enough to have the best manager in the business. More than that, we had a club spirit which started with chairman Bob Kelly and his directors and ran right through to the youngest boy on the groundstaff.

Celtic, of course, have great traditions. They have always treated their players well and I was aware of this long before we won the European Cup. But in the close season after our victory in Lisbon something happened which made me realize why Celtic are a great club. I think you will realize exactly what I mean when I tell you a story which has never been told before.

I should explain in the first place that the Boss does not believe in the 'star system' in football. He recognizes that every team will have an outstanding player or maybe even two or three, but he maintains they are only valuable as long as they contribute to the team effort. He left no doubt in our minds that the team was more important than any individual and I know he often discouraged Press men from picking out individuals for praise. Off the field he liked us to do things together, as a team.

At the end of last season, therefore, when it came to the time for re-signing, most members of the first-team pool had some sort of grouse. Although we had won everything as a team and done everything as a team we knew one player was being paid quite a bit more than the rest of us. That didn't seem right—and talking to the other boys I got the impression they would not re-sign until this was sorted out.

Shortly before I was due to go on holiday the Boss called me into his office and told me I was the only player who had not re-signed. I wasn't too surprised, because in football you will always find players who do a lot of moaning in the bath, but when the moment comes when they should speak up they have nothing to say. I expect this happens in all walks of life. Anyway, I told Mr. Stein that I would not re-sign as long as one player was getting more than the rest of us. I said I thought it was a fair principle that if we were all equal then we should be paid accordingly. I also pointed out how often he had told us we were all equal in the Celtic team.

He seemed sympathetic and assured me that the contract which gave the other player a bigger wage had been signed before he (the Boss) had come to Parkhead as manager. He asked me what my terms were for re-signing, and I said I wanted £10 per week more.

A couple of days later I was back in the Boss's office where he told me the Board had decided they could not agree to my request.

So I went off on holiday without re-signing and when I came back I joined the Players' Union and took legal advice about my position. At that time 'keeper Jim Cruickshank of Hearts was having similar difficulties. His was something of a test case and, as I remember, it was ruled that he could play

for the club as long as he was registered with the S.F.A.,
even if he had not re-signed. The difference between the two
of us was that while he wanted a transfer I had no desire at all
to leave Parkhead. The days passed and I was included in the
team against Tottenham in our pre-season friendly which
was played at Hampden Park. We had won the Scottish Cup;
Spurs were the F.A. Cup holders; and this was a terrific
match which I enjoyed. I would have enjoyed it more, however, if my re-signing problems had been solved. The newspapers until then had made little of my differences with the
club, simply because they had been told little about it. At the
back of my mind I knew I didn't want it to become a big
issue and it was a temptation to re-sign and forget about the
£10. Yet I felt strongly that my principle was right and I
ought to stick by it.

Then, on the Saturday night after the game with Spurs, the
Boss told me to report at Parkhead the following morning at
eleven o'clock. He didn't say why he wanted me there . . . but
I was pretty sure it wasn't for an extra training stint!

When I got to Parkhead I found that my appointment was
not with the Boss, but with the Chairman of Celtic, Bob Kelly
himself. Mr. Kelly can be quite an imposing figure, but I
found him easy to talk to and this proved to be a friendly and
frank discussion. I told him I thought it was reasonable to ask
for a rise if another player was getting more than I was and I
added that if the club wanted to make some private arrange-
ment to pay me the money I would not go around telling
other players. It was up to them, after all, to make their own
wage arrangements.

Mr. Kelly made it clear early in the conversation that he
tried to have players of character in his club and if I had been
a troublemaker who was likely to go on making demands of
all kinds then he would not want me at Parkhead. As it was,
he said he did not want to break up the team which had won
the European Cup. At the same time he did not think it would
be fair to give me a rise and hide it from the others.

As we talked on I realized why the man who had often been called 'Mr. Celtic' had such a good reputation among former players. His chief concern was to have all his players happy and to treat them fairly. The time flew. We actually talked for about two hours and then he made the proposition which staggered me.

He said the Board had agreed to give me the rise, but there would be nothing underhand about it. All the other players in the pool, except the one who was being paid more, would get the same as myself. Then he asked me if I was satisfied. I was delighted, naturally. I had been given exactly what I asked for and that was all that concerned me. If the other players had benefited too, well and good.

It was as I drove home that day, however, that I fully realized what a tremendous gesture this was by the club. They could have said I was a nuisance, put me on the transfer list, and finished up with a fair sum in the bank. They could have given me the rise, told me to keep quiet about it, and the cost would have been only about £500 in the year. Instead, in order to keep faith with their players, they chose the costliest way out of all. Because with a pool of around fifteen players Mr. Kelly committed himself that Sunday morning to an extra wage bill of £7,500 in the year!

Most clubs would have found an easier way out. But this is undoubtedly where part of Celtic's greatness lies. Their treatment of players is second to none and in recent seasons I'm sure our wages at Parkhead have compared well with the top teams in England's First Division. We are also given a seaside break from training, when fixtures permit, more often than most clubs.

All these things make players contented and create a happy atmosphere in the dressing-room. But this does not necessarily give you a winning team. That's where manager Jock Stein comes in. Since he arrived at Parkhead in 1965 we have had fantastic success. I've already said I think he is the best manager in the business. And people are always asking me

what makes him so different from the rest. There are a lot of
reasons, but I think the most important is a little trick he has
for getting the best out of players. He never tells you how
good you are, nor talks about your strong points. He simply
reminds you of the things you do badly.

He may say to one player: 'Listen, you leave the shooting to
someone else. I don't expect you to be the leading scorer.' Or
he may tell another: 'Every time you carry the ball you
get into trouble. Concentrate on finding a man with a pass
and the game will be a lot easier.' As a result of this kind of
advice everyone at Celtic Park makes fewer mistakes than
he used to do, because we are all avoiding the things we do
badly.

Our teamwork has also improved because the Boss has
laid down a pattern of play which takes the guesswork out of
the game. If, for instance, I move forward for a shot I know
what my left-half is doing and I know where our left-winger
will go. Everyone has a job to do and as long as they do it the
game is simple.

As I've mentioned in earlier chapters the Boss has a great
sense of humour and in his best moods will joke as much as
anyone at training. Yet he is a strict disciplinarian. I love to
try a crafty back-heeler from time to time, but if one of them
goes astray and exposes the defence I have to prepare for
a verbal lacing at half-time or after the game. Everyone
is treated alike by the Boss. While wee Jimmy Johnstone
is accepted as the star of the present side, he knows that
if he turns up late for training he is liable to be sent home
again and told to return in the afternoon to train on his own.
It has happened before and no doubt it will happen again!

In our training sessions at the Barrowfield ground he will
allow a certain amount of larking about then, without warning, he'll clamp down on it. 'All right, that's enough,' he'll
say, and then we know we are on our way back to slog round
the track at Parkhead. Our practice matches at Parkhead can
be deadly serious and if two players clash and take too long

to patch their quarrel then the Boss will step in, stop the game, and send us all back to lap the track.

In present-day football peak fitness is essential. The Boss has never left us in any doubt about that and many people agree that our fitness was a key factor in most matches we played during our European Cup run. We are as fit as any team, therefore, and the Boss makes sure we stay that way. Every now and again he will turn to trainer Neilly Mochan and say: 'I think we should do a bit extra this morning, eh? Let's work really hard today.'

A 'bit extra' means that Mochan can put us through his most demanding routines until lunch-time. It's a test of stamina and everything else. No matter how fit you are these sessions stretch you to the limit. They serve a very important purpose, of course, because during the season many players, at one time or another, are tempted to break from their routine of sensible eating and quiet living. They will still be basically fit and on a normal training day get through the various exercises without difficulty. But on a day when we do a 'bit extra' the Boss knows he will have no difficulty spotting anyone who has been enjoying himself too much. Their 'distress signals' will be only too obvious. He won't have to warn them either because they will have learned their lesson painfully that morning.

Nobody takes liberties with the Boss, therefore, because you know he is sure to find you out—and since you know the punishment is liable to be severe you don't take the risk in the first place.

4

How I hit Them

LAST year the *Sunday Mirror* ran a competition to find the player in Scottish football who hit the ball hardest. I was as surprised as anyone when I won it. They said my shots travelled at a fraction under seventy miles per hour!

It's nice to know you can hit a ball hard, but I rather wish I had discovered it before I was twenty-one. Yes, it was only when the Boss encouraged me to start playing the over-lapping full-back type of game that I began to think of hitting the ball hard. But wait, before I go on I must tell you how over-lapping almost got me the sack at Celtic Park.

Before the Boss took over at Parkhead I heard a whisper that he would be leaving Hibs to join us. I remembered that while he was with Dunfermline I had been told that he liked attacking full-backs. So I thought I would do a little bit of self-projection. Until then, like every other full-back in Scotland, my job had been to tackle hard and belt the ball forward. But off my own bat I started moving upfield, so that when Mr. Stein arrived he would spot me as ideal material. I was an ambitious lad at twenty-one!

There was one Celtic official, however, who did not think much of my attempts to join the attack. He advised me against it, but I still slipped forward a few times in the next match. So then he warned me that if I wandered from my position again I would be out of the team. Fortunately, the Boss took over soon after this and my inclination to attack got his blessing. And, as I say, that was when the shooting began.

In my schooldays I had been a fairly ordinary inside- or outside-right with no knack for grabbing goals. In those days I was about average height too and then, from when I was about fifteen until I was eighteen, I really began to sprout. Maybe that was why Celtic spotted me. In those days I was playing for Wishaw School team in the Saturday mornings and Meadow Thistle Amateurs in the afternoons. After that I was farmed out to Coltness United, but even as a junior I still couldn't shoot. In fact, the only time they asked me to take a penalty I scooped it high over the bar.

Under the Boss's guidance, however, I began to try a shot when I was upfield. Much to my surprise I began to find I was hitting the ball quite hard. During training he would give me extra spells of shooting practice until I could make a reasonable job of a shot with either foot. Now, I even have the feeling I hit the ball better with my left, although I never thought of myself as a left-footer.

I know some people will read this and think that a big bloke like me ought to be able to hit the ball hard. Yet I am convinced that height and weight have nothing to do with how well you strike the ball. Shooting in football is the same as driving in golf. The power comes from the timing—and I must be lucky enough to have a kick which contacts at the right moment. I know plenty of big blokes, after all, who could hardly burst a paper bag.

Yet a player who used to be at Parkhead a few years ago called Bobby Jeffrey had one of the hardest shots I've ever seen. Bobby was only about 5 ft. 5 ins., but his timing must have been terrific. I would think, therefore, that anyone who wanted to have a big shot in football could do so simply by working at it until he got the timing right.

In the last couple of seasons my ability to belt the ball has also got me the job as Celtic's penalty-taker. Now I know that somebody somewhere is sure to be wondering what the secret is for successful penalty-taking. Well, it's quite simple. You just run up and give the ball a terrible dunt!

This, of course, is another part of my game which I have only developed in the past eighteen months or so. In my young days I took no more than anyone else and, as I've said, I

This proves there's harmony between 'Old Firm' players! We were making a record with comedians Jimmy Logan and Larry Marshall

We get around a lot with Celtic, but as you can see from our expressions there's no fun in waiting for transport

A typical airport gathering for the photographers, but this one was special because the man in the middle of the back row is the great Alfredo di Stefano

All set for shooting . . . with a gun and a dog. I'm the one in the middle

I'm trying to console Kai Johansen after he missed a penalty in a League Cup-tie with Rangers. But I don't know what Billy Johnston is saying to Bobby Lennox

Billy McNeill and I get a close-up view of a Bobby Charlton shot which didn't go into the net in this year's Scotland–England game

A Rangers attack is broken up and Ronnie Simpson goes down to
collect in another 'Old Firm' game

A typical action shot of myself at a training session

missed on the only occasion Coltness gave me the job to do. But there was one time when I was the unemployed penalty king of Parkhead!

It was about four years ago. Celtic had been missing one or two penalties, so a little competition was arranged during training to find out which of the first-team players had the best technique for spotkicks. I was in great form that morning. I think I scored with twelve out of twelve. Nobody came near me and I was elected official penalty-taker. I was quite pleased with myself and looking forward to taking my first kick in public. But two months passed without a referee ever pointing to the spot. Then we had another competition during training. I was the worst in the team. I think I sank only one in about ten attempts. From that moment I was sacked from the penalty-taking job . . . before I had even one kick in earnest.

Since I began taking them again, however, in the season before last, I have only missed about two—and these misses taught me a lesson. They showed why you must be thinking all the time in First Division football.

I'll explain what I mean. There are two ways of taking a penalty kick. You can stroke the ball carefully, trying to place it as far away from the 'keeper as possible. Or you can use the 'terrible dunt' method. If a goalkeeper throws himself in the right direction he will probably save the first kind of kick because the ball is not travelling fast and so is easily deflected.

With the second method the 'keeper should have no chance unless you shoot straight at him. If he dives and gets a hand or an arm to the ball, the power of the shot will still carry it over the line in most cases. A 'keeper's only chance, therefore, is to move before the kick is taken and hope to get his body in the line of fire—and after taking penalties for about a year I began to realize this was happening. The good goalkeepers, knowing I always hammered the ball, were taking a chance and moving along the line as I ran up to take the kick. They knew the kick would be retaken if the referee spotted them, but this is a trick which a ref. can often miss. There was one game anyway where I took a penalty and when the ball struck the 'keeper's leg he was practically at the post. He had obviously moved, but as the ref. let him away with it I knew it was time I found my own remedy.

The next three times I placed my shots and scored easily as the 'keeper's were obviously expecting a full-blooded drive. Today I vary my penalties according to which 'keeper I'm facing, but I'm still convinced the best way to score from the spot is give the ball a terrible dunt!

5

Against England!

I'M not a bit biased. I just don't care who beats England!

That's a typical Scottish attitude which, I know, doesn't make a lot of sense to anyone else. It doesn't make much sense to me either, but I'm stuck with it. I think I must have been born with this feeling, like a lot of other Scots, because although I have several good friends who are English I have to admit that as a nation they constantly annoy me.

In football this anti-English feeling reaches a peak once every year when we meet the 'Auld Enemy' at either Hampden or Wembley. While it is an honour to play for your country in any game, I'm sure most players value a 'cap' against England much more than against any other country. And, of course, the greatest international thrill is to be in a Scottish side which beats England. Apart from the terrific feeling of satisfaction you have personally, you know that Scots in their thousands all over the country are as happy as you are at that moment.

I've been lucky enough to play three times against England, but the game I'll never forget was the one in which we beat them 3-2 at Wembley in 1967. They were the World champions. We were the team who hadn't even qualified for the world finals. But that day at Wembley we took the shine off their crown. It was their first defeat since they had won the title—and let me say right now that the man who can take almost all the credit for humbling them then is Jim Baxter.

Before I go on I should explain I wasn't always a Baxter fan. In Ranger's light blue jersey he was a bogy to Celtic as he was to any other club in the Scottish League. With his uncanny control and inch-perfect passes he could make

Rangers play as he wanted and in the inevitable victory Slim Jim was a self-confident, arrogant so-and-so.

At Wembley last year, however, I found out that while Baxter's supreme self-confidence could irritate the opposition, it could also inspire his own team . . . and we needed all the inspiration we could get in the build-up to that match. England, with their full team, were playing on the field where they won their World title. They were, quite rightly, red-hot favourites.

We were an unknown quantity—and it was very difficult to make out a case for us.

Ronnie Simpson, in goal, was making his international debut at thirty-six and inside-forward Jim McCalliog from Sheffield Wednesday was another newcomer. Jimmy Johnstone had called off through injury and Bobby Lennox, Willie Wallace, and myself did not have a lot of international experience among us. Even the manager, Bobby Brown, had only been in the job a matter of weeks—and as we didn't travel to London until two days before the game there was not a great deal he could do. He was actually meeting some of the players for the first time only.

But from the moment we all met in our London headquarters it was Baxter who put us in the right frame of mind. He had such a glorious contempt for the English team that we all began to think the same way. If anyone tried to indicate a strong point in the England team Jim brushed it aside with his strong Fife accent and a few characteristic phrases which I won't detail, as his vocabulary can be a bit colourful.

Denis Law, in a quieter sort of way, also helped us to see the English team in proportion. What impressed me about Law was his determination to win. He told me: 'It's all right for you blokes. Win or lose you go back to Scotland and soon forget it. But if we are beaten they won't let me forget it down here for months after.'

As far as this game was concerned my troubles really began when we were taken on the Friday to see Wembley itself. I had never been there before, although I had watched games from there on the telly. When I saw how perfect the pitch was and looked at the stands all around, I imagined what like it would be with 100,000 people in them and I began to think about how it would feel to have a bad game in front of that lot. I got a real attack of the jitters—and I wasn't feeling too cool the next day either. I remember my mother and father came round to see me outside the dressing-room before the game began. I was signing a youngster's autograph book when my mother asked: 'Are you feeling all right?' I said: 'Great, great,' as convincingly as I could. So she gave me a long look then whispered: 'You're as white as a ghost.'

Frankly, I felt white too. I was a bag of nerves and inside the dressing-room I could see that, although he had played there three times in F.A. Cup Finals, Ronnie Simpson was also having a job to relax. Then I looked at Baxter. He was lying flat on his back on one of the bench seats as if he hadn't a care in the world. What a cool customer he is! Yet at that moment I had a pretty good idea what he was thinking about.

In that morning's *Daily Express*, sports writer Desmond Hackett, who loves to annoy the Scots whenever he can, had written a really cheeky piece. His point was that the game was a waste of time really and that we had a cheek coming over the border to tangle with the World Champions. He made it clear we were going to get a hiding.

Jim was furious when he read it. Apart from a few choice words about the writer he said: 'Wait till we get out there. I'll give Hackett something to write about. If we're leading, I'll show him how good his World champions are.' We all resented Hackett's article, but Jim acted as if it was a personal challenge.

There had been no time for elaborate plans and manager Brown simply asked as to do the same job for him as we did for our clubs. But Baxter gave more than he could give for a club. He was playing against England and he had made up his mind they were going to be beaten. With the ball at his feet he was king . . . and he made sure everyone knew it. For my own part I got the ball away from Jimmy Greaves twice in the early minutes and after that my nerves disappeared. Everyone else had settled quickly too and before very long it was obvious the game was going our way.

Mark you, I was not too happy on one occasion when I toddled upfield and Ray Wilson tackled me. The studs of his boot caught the top of my foot and one was above the level of my boot. That was a sore one and I had to sit down outside the touchline as trainer Walter McCrae got to work. As the pain eased I looked up . . . just in time to see Denis Law prodding the ball home. Scotland were one up!

'Okay, Walter, it's fine now,' I shouted, and raced back on to the field. It's a funny thing, but no matter how good the trainer may be, nothing gets rid of pain better than the sight of the opening goal in a game like that.

It put the seal on the fact that we were the better team and we held the lead until the interval . . . but by then every Englishman had his excuse ready. In the first half centre-half Jackie Charlton had been injured and since then all of them, including Sir Alf Ramsey, have used this to explain away the defeat of the World champions that day at Wembley. Well, I didn't feel a bit sorry for the big Leeds United man then, and I don't now. Yes, I know he broke his toe and actually managed to be England's best forward in the second half, but I still can't shed a tear for him. I'll tell you why.

In my opinion the tackle which caused his injury was a desperate and dangerous one. Bobby Lennox was really flying down the left wing when the big fellow charged across. He mistimed his run and I don't think he had any chance of making contact with the ball. But he sailed in anyway and down came Lennox. There was such an impact that one of the studs in Charlton's boot actually broke in Bobby's knee, leaving a nasty hole. The other half of the stud was pushed inside the centre-half's boot and that was how his big toe was broken.

Charlton, of course, has had a lot of praise for playing on, although he did not realize then the toe was broken. But how much praise has Bobby Lennox had? He had to go on running and chasing for the rest of the match with that hole in his leg and he still managed to score in the second half. Bobby got no credit for his courage, because to my knowledge the English Press never bothered to go into any detail about the reason for Charlton's injury. It seems to me if the force of the tackle was enough to break a stud, then Bobby was lucky not to get a much more serious injury, although the cut was bad enough.

That Lennox goal after the interval put us two ahead—and that was when Jim Baxter turned on the style. He had silently promised Mr. Hackett an exhibition, and he gave him it. As soon as he saw we were in a strong position, Jim began going down to the penalty-box every time Ronnie Simpson got the ball and shouting: 'Pit the ba' at ma feet.' This hadn't been part of Ronnie's pre-match instructions, but since he was a new boy in the team he didn't argue and tried to oblige Baxter as often as he could. With a virtual monopoly of the ball the slim one dictated the game completely. Sometimes he stopped play altogether; sometimes he did a bit of juggling; and at all times he taunted the World champions in the cheekiest manner possible. This was Baxter in a class of his own. I can think of no other player, of any nationality, who would have dared to treat England as he did before so many of their own followers in Wembley Stadium of all places.

I bet every Scot who looked on enjoyed Jim's showmanship as much as I did, yet he came in for criticism later. Although we won 3–2, with Jim McCalliog getting our other goal. Jackie Charlton and Geoff Hurst were able to score at the other end and some people thought Baxter's determination to 'take the mickey' gave England a chance to save the game when we ought to have been banging on the goals and giving them a hammering. I agree. I'm sure we could have bagged more goals in the second half if we had put our minds to it. But this is how it is with Baxter. You have to take him the way you get him.

I imagine any manager who has ever had Jim in his team would agree with me. I can, of course, only speak from my experience with the Scottish team. I've watched Walter McCrae get red in the face trying to get 'J.B.' to do an exercise EXACTLY the same way as everyone else. The more serious Walter became the more outrageous Jim behaved. I'm well aware this is not the way an international footballer should carry on. Yet on these occasions I was a neutral. I realized that Walter had a reputation as a top-class trainer to protect. But I knew too that Jim was just as determined to preserve his reputation as a 'character'. You see, he just can't resist a bit of mischief.

I can remember a typical example of this before that Wembley game. A young photographer called Brian Morgan from the *Daily Record* in Glasgow was in London to cover the big game. It was a big assignment for him and in honour of the occasion he was wearing what looked like his 'Sunday suit'. One of his jobs was to get a picture of the Scottish team in a group together on the Wembley pitch. I had noticed before that he loves to get an angle on his picture and sure enough he went down on one knee for this shot. Before he could move the shutter, however, a voice with a strong Fife accent said: 'Wait a minute, son. Yer too near. Awa' back a bit.'

This was a bit of advice young Brian could have done without. But he obviously decided it was better to humour Baxter rather than take the chance of him refusing to pose. So he went back a few inches. 'Naw, naw, a bit further,' coaxed Jim. This went on for a couple of minutes until 'J.B.' indicated he was satisfied. Brian, a little perturbed, took his picture. Then, as he stood up, the truth dawned on him.

Scotland's irrepressible left-half had not been concerned about the quality of the picture. He had simply been easing his victim back until he was on the touchline. As a result there was a vivid white stripe right across the photographer's navy blue trousers. I don't know how long it took Brian to rub off the stain, but I do know the expression on his face was priceless.

And speaking of expressions on faces. . . . That brings me back to the game itself and the members of that beaten English team. It was a great victory for us. It made us favourites to reach the quarter-finals of the European Nations Cup the following year. And since England had the World Cup safely in their cupboard you might think they would not grudge us our moment of glory, especially since they have the reputation for being better losers than we are!

Well I can tell you that reputation was badly tarnished in London's Café Royal where the after-match banquet was held. At the informal get-together before the meal England captain Bobby Moore sat in a corner and gave the distinct impression that he wanted nothing to do with the smiling Scots in the room. As far as I could see several of the others were just as reluctant to fraternize. Sir Alf Ramsey also did not look too pleased and when S.F.A. President Tom Reid made a couple of characteristic wisecracks the England boss did not appear amused.

Some of the other England boys, however, made a point of congratulating us over a beer. Nobby Stiles, Alan Ball, and Bobby Charlton were very friendly and that goes for Jackie Charlton too! Even if I didn't like his tackle on Bobby Lennox, I can assure you Jackie is a great guy off the field. Like his brother, he is likeable, natural, and thoroughly down-to-earth. With all their success, the Charltons have not even the slightest tendency towards being bigheads.

I don't expect I need remind you that in our other British Championship matches last year the Scottish team never recaptured the Wembley form and so we arrived at the return game with England in February of this year needing an out-right win at Hampden to stay in the European Nations Cup. Logically, this should have been easy enough for a team that

D

had won at Wembley, but it wasn't nearly as simple as that.

In fact, manager Bobby Brown's problems multiplied day by day as the Hampden game approached. Jim Baxter and Jim McCalliog had lost form; Denis Law was having trouble with an old knee injury; and even when he named a 'pool' of players the Scotland manager had to cut it quickly as English clubs were pressing him for the use of players. Frankly, I was pleasantly surprised to find myself in the party of fourteen players who finally went to Largs to prepare for the big game at Hampden.

I felt I had not been playing too well previously and some of the newspapers had hinted that Rangers' John Greig might be given No. 2 jersey. Nevertheless, as it turned out, I got my third 'cap' against England—and I'm certainly not complaining about Mr. Brown's choice.

Looking back now at the Hampden game I can see that things were always going against Scotland and fate obviously never intended us to win. Even at Largs, John Hughes was troubled with a leg injury which was slow to clear and then, less than 48 hours before the kick-off, Spurs' Alan Gilzean called off after straining himself in a practice match.

This was a big blow. He was the key striker in our plans. Quite apart from his ability to grab goals, however, 'Gilly' is a big help to a defence. If you are under pressure, you know you can skelp a high ball up the middle and rely on him to tame it or flick it on with his head to someone else. As Peter Cormack of Hibs was called in as a replacement for Gilzean there was a possibility of switching all our tactics as these players' styles are totally different. The day before the game Mr. Brown gathered us together in the gym of the Largs Recreation Centre and told us John Hughes would have a fitness test the following morning. If he passed he would play, if not Cormack was in. In that same talk the manager told us right-winger Jimmy Johnstone would definitely not play as he was 'not mentally attuned' for the match. It was made clear then that this was a strictly confidential bit of information which must not be passed outside the Scottish camp.

But someone leaked that information and the newspapers made quite a thing of it. This was a pity, because such a snippet of information did no more than baffle the fans. They could not understand how a player could be 'not mentally attuned'. I understood only too well.

It so happens that, like many great players, wee Jimmy is a highly temperamental bloke. To get the best out of him you have to have him in the right mood when he goes on the field. At Parkhead the Boss is a master at keeping Jimmy's pecker up because he understands the wee man and knows how he will react. Few people, in fact, understand him as well. Scotland trainer Walter McCrae, for instance, could hardly have such knowledge, and that was why he was unlucky enough to make a *faux pas* in that week at Largs. Before a practice match against Celtic, who were staying along the coast at Seamill, he asked Jimmy to act as linesman. It must have seemed logical to Walter as Jimmy had not been named in the team for Hampden. Knowing him, I can imagine how the wee man reacted. In any event, he made it clear he did not want to be a linesman.

Walter couldn't possibly know that it was unthinkable for Jimmy to run the line in that game. You see, his greatest chums at Parkhead are Bobby Lennox and Willie O'Neil. They get on like a house on fire and kid each other mercilessly. If Jimmy had run the line with the other two playing in the match his life wouldn't have been worth living when he got back to Parkhead!

Quite apart from this, I suspect almost any world-class player would rebel, as Johnstone did, at the idea of being used as a linesman.

I think that the story is interesting, nevertheless it shows how difficult life can be for the men in charge of an international squad. Unless they can keep the same group of players together for a long series of matches they can't hope to get to know them really well. Yet if they don't have that kind of knowledge then an incident like the one I have just told you about can happen quite easily.

On the morning of the England game John Hughes, better known at Parkhead as 'the Bear', passed his test. As he could play a similar role to 'Gilly' we had no problems with tactics. At least, not in theory anyway, but at Hampden we found we had plenty of problems. England needed only a draw to clinch their place in the European Nations Cup semi-finals . . . and they were rarely in danger of failing. I hate to say that, but there's no point in hiding from the truth.

England actually scored first with a great shot by Martin Peters and the only time we ever looked like winning was for a short spell before the interval after 'the Bear' had headed an equalizer. We had Ramsey's boys pinned back, but we never opened them up because I don't think we had the players to do it. It might have been quite a different story, however, if Jim Baxter had been playing. With England always ready to fall back Jim could have had a field day. But he wasn't chosen because he was badly off form and nobody can argue with that, as manager Brown would have been severely criticized if Baxter had flopped in such a vital game.

Yet I must admit I would never leave Jim out of a Scottish team as long as we were playing England. As I've already tried to explain, beating England means everything to Baxter, as it does to me and so many other Scots. Against other countries, I admit, he is liable to play as if he couldn't care less, but never when he sees those white English jerseys in front of him. No matter how much he might be off form for his club. Even if he wasn't in peak physical condition. Even if he could play only half-a-game or half-an-hour I would put Baxter in Scotland's team against England this year, next year, and probably for as long as he is able to shout: 'Pit the ba' at ma feet!'

Another player who might have opened up that English defence was Jimmy Johnstone. But then he might not have got the chance. The predictions were that this game would be a 'kicking match' and the one sure way to stop Jimmy would have been to chop him down.

As it was, they did not have to do much kicking because they were never seriously threatened. If they had been I'm sure the game would have been rough because listening to the Anglo-Scots in our party talking before this game I reached the conclusion that most players down south seem to be obsessed by the physical side of the game. They seem to talk so much of 'playing it hard' and 'giving stick' I can't help thinking players down there must be judged by how hard they can kick. Billy Bremner of Leeds was certainly a handy man when it came to warning us which players in the England squad were most likely to kick.

One Englishman Bremner had the greatest admiration for, however, was West Ham's Geoff Hurst. Said Billy: 'I've found from my own experience—and other players agree with me—that no matter how hard you tackle Hurst he just gives himself a shake and goes on playing. Then just to show you haven't frightened him he comes back later and gives you as much as he got!'

After the Hampden game I can now testify that everything Billy said about Hurst is true. During the first half I had occasion to challenge Hurst and with all my weight behind me I expected to brush him aside. Instead, I got the feeling I had just run into a double-decker bus. Yes, Hurst is a very well-made fellow. Later in the second half we clashed near the touchline and he caught me a kick on the back of the calf. It was a real 'beauty' and I pushed down my stocking to ease the pain. I pushed the other one down too because I thought I would look a Charlie with one up and one down.

That was a mistake. Next day the Scottish critics were writing that 'Gemmell tired badly in the second half' and 'Gemmell ran out of stamina' or remarks like that. They had spotted the stockings down and decided I had cramp or was just too tired to care. We had failed to win. They were looking for fall guys . . . and I was one of them.

In fact, let me take the chance to slip in this point about Scotland's football writers. It seems to me they tend to go to extremes. If you win you're wonderful. But if you lose—heaven help you. There are no half-measures with our critics. Perhaps this is not a bad thing, but when a player is having a poor game he does not need the point hammered home. He knows only too well himself.

And having got that off my chest, I think perhaps this is a good time to make another couple of points which seem to me quite important.

I think, for instance, too many people overlook the fact that Anglo-Scots have a great advantage over Scottish League players in these internationals. They are, after all, playing against their English opponents week in week out down south. They see them have their good games, and their bad ones, and when they face them on the international field they know exactly what to expect. If you are playing in Scotland all season, however, your knowledge of the England players is liable to be based mainly on glowing reports you have read in the newspapers.

I think this tends to make the England stars seem far greater players then they really are and so it is easy to be overawed when you come face to face with them for the first time.

It seems to me, of course, that all players in England's First Division are depicted a little larger than life—and this applies to the Scots down south as much as to anyone else. Because someone is playing well for an English side this does not necessarily make him a better player than a bloke who has never crossed the border. Nevertheless, a lot of people seem to think so.

Let's take the case of Billy Bremner, for instance. Nobody would dispute he is a good player. He's got lots of guts. He has amazing stamina for his size and he does a terrific job for

Leeds United. Yet if Billy was using all that guts and stamina in Scotland I wonder if people would rave about him so much. He is, after all, a destructive player. He's an inspiration to Leeds in helping them not to lose games, but he doesn't really have the ability to go through and win a match.

Because of this, I reckon we have a player at Parkhead who is streets ahead of Bremner as a creative wing-half, yet he never gets half the praise which is showered on the Leeds man. Yes, I'm thinking of Bobby Murdoch. If Bobby was playing down south he would be hailed as a super half-back. As well as being strong in the tackle he repeatedly brings the ball through to make goals—and he can score them too with a much stronger shot than Bremner. Yet when internationals come around, even here in Scotland, people start talking of Bremner, the less creative of the two.

In this particular case I think Murdoch may be at a disadvantage because of the type of game Celtic play. We are an attacking team, always going for goals.

If we have a big win, therefore, it is the forwards who make the headlines. No matter how well a half-back may play in any game, he is unlikely to get more than a passing mention if the men in front of him have scored six goals! So even at his best Bobby is in danger of being overlooked.

This wouldn't happen, however, if he was playing for Leeds. They have a pretty ordinary attack and so it is the half-back line which carries the burden of the work. Right-half Billy, with his bright red hair, is invariably in the thick of the midfield fight and so has the opportunity to command attention.

He is an invaluable player for Leeds, yet I think it is fair to say he has not had a super game for Scotland. In my view this is because Billy is basically a destroyer and the international arena will always be dominated by the creative player.

This is why I believe that if Bobby Murdoch, with his great goal-making ability, had been playing in English football during recent years he would have had a great deal more recognition. He might also have had the chance to wear a Scottish jersey much more often than he has done. Bobby, of course, is perfectly happy at Parkhead and if he doesn't always get as much credit as he should he is certainly appreciated by those of us who are lucky enough to be playing alongside him.

While I've used Murdoch and Bremner as an ideal example, I believe there will always be instances where a Scottish League player has as much ability as an Anglo-Scot yet fails to get anything like the recognition.

Well, I've had my say on these points . . . so now we can get back to that game at Hampden. Actually, there is not a great deal more to be said about it. A 1–1 draw put us out of the European Nations Cup, but it was not such a bad result considering the difficulties which occurred before the game through players not being available and others getting injuries. England showed again that, if nothing else, they are a well-drilled team and Geoff Hurst certainly convinced me he is the toughest player in British football.

And I'll remember the game for the brilliance of Bobby Charlton and the way he really took the mickey out of me on one occasion. He had been strolling around in midfield doing pretty much as he liked when I decided it was time to show him. As he came through with the ball I charged in, determined to make a spectacular clearance. But suddenly there was no ball, no Charlton, and all I did was lose my balance bundling thin air.

What happened was that Charlton had seen me coming, pulled the ball back at the last minute, and did one of the marvellous little turnabouts of his while I flew past. More than that, as I missed him, he raised one hand a little and shouted 'Olé.' I was probably the only one who heard him shout and I couldn't help laughing because a bullfighter could not have side-stepped more neatly than Bobby did at that moment. The incident also showed how completely in

Bobby Moore, England's
captain, leads his team on to
the field

Billy Bremner, Leeds,
throws up an arm in
triumph after scoring against
Chelsea

Jackie Charlton, Leeds, in action against Newcastle

Manchester United's George Best in a tussel with Storey of Arsenal

Johnstone, myself, Rooney and Mochan celebrate after our
Scottish Cup victory against Aberdeen

St. Johnstone left-winger Wilson is outnumbered as I nod one
back to Ronnie Simpson with Billy McNeill standing by

Billy McNeill goes up for a corner against Partick Thistle—and this shows how high Billy gets up

It's a goal . . . from Stevie Chalmers (*right*) against Hearts

command of himself this great player must be when he can think of a gag in the heat of a game like that.

We clashed again later in the game and Bobby got a bit of a knock, but he is a terrific sport and we had a good old natter later at the big banquet.

The only other story relating to the Hampden game, or rather the preliminaries, shows that wee Jimmy Johnstone has a sense of humour too. It was a week after the match with England. Celtic were at Rugby Park for a League game with Kilmarnock and we really struck form. Well, maybe I should say wee Jimmy was at his best. He tore the Killie defence apart on his own and caused so much havoc we finished up with a handsome six-goal win. Then as we walked off in a very happy frame of mind at the finish, the wee man spotted trainer Walter McCrea and shouted: 'Not bad for a linesman, eh Walter?'

It was a pretty sharp quip which I'm sure the Kilmarnock man saw the funny side of too.

Football, of course, is full of these kind of wisecracks which the public rarely hear about. In fact, although it might appear to be a serious game there are gags flying all the time and I find that most players have a quick sense of humour. In fact, if the remarks in some matches were all taken down on a tape-recorder they might be more entertaining than the football itself. Maybe then the fans might not get as emotional as they are liable to do in the games I want to talk about next.

6

Willie Henderson and I

WILLIE HENDERSON and I are the best of pals. I can honestly say we have always got on well together. This is probably because we have a similar sense of humour and every time we meet we take the mickey out of each other. Willie says terrible things about this nose of mine just because it happens to be a shade larger than the average, and I get my own back by gagging about him being short-sighted. I always throw in the odd remark about his broken nose. Although when I do that he usually says: 'If you ever break that nose of yours you won't be able to see your ears, sur!'

I'm telling you about our cross-talk because I know many people will be surprised. There are lots of Rangers supporters, for instance, who think we are deadly enemies.

It isn't difficult, of course, to realize why they think that way. Willie has been Rangers' right-winger for some years now. I've been Celtic's left-back pretty regularly. And since the 'Old Firm' are probably the most famous football rivals in the world Willie and I have to be on opposite sides of the fence. In fact, I've always played against the wee man in many 'Old Firm' clashes and you can be sure we were determined to beat each other every time.

One snag is that I'm a lot bigger bloke than Willie and so every time he goes down in a tackle I look like a villain. But Rangers supporters don't call me a villain. . . . They've got a much stronger term. In fact, starting about eighteen months ago about twenty or thirty thousand of them never missed a chance during 'Old Firm' matches to chant: 'Gemmell is a ——.' I'm not going to print the word here because it is not the kind anyone would use in front of women, children, or indeed at any time. I think it is true to say that Rangers officials, and everyone else in football, have been shocked by this chant.

Many people ask me how it feels when thousands of people roar in unison, 'Gemmell is a ——.' Well, I admit it was a bit of a shaker the first time I heard it, but now it doesn't really upset me. I've come to the conclusion that if I have roused Rangers followers that much then I must have played well against their team. If I had played badly they would have ignored me. I dare say this kind of thing is liable to happen in matches involving Celtic and Rangers where the feelings of the crowd are so strong.

It is even more obvious my clashes with Willie Henderson have had a lot to do with it. To the man on the terracing there must have been many a time when it seemed as if I was too rough on Willie. Yet I can tell you, one bloke who doesn't think so is the wee man himself. In fact, it is not so very long since he came to my defence.

A bunch of Rangers and Celtic players were gathered together before a representative game. The conversation came round to wingers and how they were kicked, and then a Rangers player said: 'Watch it, we'd better not say any more or we'll make big Tam blush, for he's kicked Willie a few times.' Before I could say a word wee Willie chimed in:

'Naw, sur, that's no fair,' he insisted. 'Tam's brought me doon many a time . . . but he disny kick me.'

Rangers supporters may take the wee winger's word for it, or there again they may not because, as I say, feelings are so strong, owing to the religious connections. Rangers are supposed to represent the Protestants and Celtic the Roman Catholics. Yet this is so silly, because the feelings exist only in the minds of the spectators. In all the 'Old Firm' games I have played in, I can remember only a couple of occasions when a player has made a remark even remotely connected with religion.

Yet the tension is terrific simply because of the attitude of the supporters. Every player knows this is one game where he dare not make a mistake. As a result, football standards are low in these games because nobody is prepared to try to be clever in case the move doesn't come off. As I've said, I'm partial to a back-heeler now and again, but I wouldn't think of trying one against Rangers in case the ball went to an opponent. Fear of mistakes destroys everyone's confidence.

Because of this I have never heard either a Rangers or Celtic player say before an 'Old Firm' game, 'We'll win.' You may think you have the better team that day; you may be optimistic; but you know it would be daft to forecast, because these games invariably hang on one slip, one careless, nervous move.

There is also the fact that there is invariably a tremendous amount at stake when the 'Old Firm' meet. A win may decide the destination of the Championship or put one of us out of the Cup. Either way there's a lot of money at stake in the long term as far as the players are concerned, so we naturally take the game very seriously. And that's another reason why I am amazed that so many fans think religion is the only thing that matters!

The players on both sides, after all, are professionals. We are out there to do a job of work and it is ridiculous to imagine we could allow any other motives to affect our play. Yet I dare say the extremists in both sets of supporters will go on thinking the worst. No matter how good a season a player may have had or how popular he may be, they will condemn him if he flops in the 'Old Firm'.

The business is crazy, of course. No wonder people in other countries laugh at the idea of mixing up religion with a football match. Yet in Glasgow it is no laughing matter—and for some players the 'Old Firm' life can be even more difficult than for others.

Yes, I'm thinking of those players, like myself, who happen to be Protestants playing for Celtic. The more fanatical supporters can't understand how this can happen. Rangers followers, particularly, think we must be some kind of traitors or fifth columnists. They can't see that if you are a youngster, mad on football, and you get a chance to sign for a famous club like Celtic . . . you grab it with both hands. You don't ask what colour of jersey you will be wearing or what church the centre-forward goes to. And now that we have won the European Cup and are firmly established as one of the most famous clubs in the world I would hate to think that any father would be so foolish as to advise his son not to sign for Celtic because of religious prejudice.

Yet I have to admit we Parkhead Protestants are most vulnerable in the 'Old Firm' games! Our mistakes are spotted by both sets of fans and our motives are always suspect. I know from experience, for instance, that if I make a bad mistake or have a poor game against Rangers then the really biased Celtic supporters who spot me in the street in the days that follow will tell me what they think of me in no uncertain terms. They will be quite convinced I was trying to help Rangers win. And on a week like that I have just as much trouble with Rangers supporters. They also think I was secretly on their side and come up, pat me on the shoulder, or give me a knowing wink, and say: 'You did a good job for us on Saturday.' Yet if I had played well these same blokes would probably be chanting 'Gemmell is a ——'.

It's crazy, it's daft, and I'm sure everybody hopes the day will soon come when these prejudices will die out in the West of Scotland. The players certainly don't encourage them. The Rangers and Celtic boys always get on well, and indeed on international trips I think they mix more with each other than they do with the Anglo-Scots.

There is even a certain amount of backchat among the boys during an 'Old Firm' game when the supporters are roaring at each other. I can remember a laugh I had with Willie Henderson as recently as this year when Rangers were at Parkhead for a League game. John Greig brought Jimmy Johnstone down with a hard tackle quite early in the game. I was standing beside Willie on the other side of the field and as we waited while Jimmy got treatment, I said solemnly: 'It looks as if things are going to get a bit tough today.' Willie looked up at me and with a deadpan expression answered: 'Ye might be right, sur, but just remember Ah'm only a wee bloke!'

I could tell you a hundred stories about the wee man because he's a great character and his short-sightedness has given us many a laugh. There was a typical incident, for instance, in the League match at Ibrox last year when we drew 2–2 and clinched the Championship. Near the end of the game Willie wanted to know the time. So he ran over towards the edge of the field, looked at the trainer's dug-out, and shouted: 'How long tae go?' Someone shouted: 'Ten minutes', and Willie ambled off into the battle again.

If, however, he had gone closer to the track and been able to recognize individuals he would have realized he was shouting into the Celtic dug-out and that the voice which answered him belonged to Jock Stein!

There was another instance too when Willie 'went over' to Celtic. We were all at a boxing show in the Central Hotel, Glasgow. The entire Celtic team had been invited as a result of our European Cup win and we had a special table with a good view of the ring. There were quite a few Rangers players there too, although their table was further back. Everything went smoothly until after the meal. As we waited for the fights to begin, I heard someone say: 'What's he doing down there?' I looked along our table and there at the end, nearest the ringside, was Willie Henderson. Some people were wondering why the Ibrox man should move into the Celtic camp. But I was sure I knew the answer. From the Rangers table, even with his glasses on, Willie would have had a hard job seeing the fighters.

As a mad keen fight fan, therefore, the wee man had decided the time had come to 'join Celtic' and get a really good view of the boxers!

I bet Willie gets his own back on me now for telling these

stories, but no matter what he says it just isn't true that when airline companies see my nose they charge me excess baggage —and I don't use table cloths for hankies.

Before I leave the subject of the 'Old Firm' I must tell you a story which never fails to amuse my friends, although it didn't seem so funny to me at the start.

As I've said already, the Rangers supporters' chant about Gemmell doesn't really upset me. But the trouble is it does not stop at Ibrox. Rangers supporters everywhere seem to know it by heart.

Some time ago my next door neighbour in Kirkintilloch started getting milk delivered from a certain dairy. The milk is delivered by young boys. As luck would have it my neighbour's delivery boy is a follower of the Light Blues . . . and he has his scarf to prove it. Now I don't know whether someone pointed out my house or whether he noticed the name himself, but it is quite a ritual with him every morning at half-past seven. After he delivers my neighbour's milk and gets to a safe distance he shouts: 'Gemmel is a ——.'

Can you imagine how it feels? While other people are awakened by the cock crowing or birds whistling, reveille for me is a squeaky Kirkintilloch voice yelling that horrible word. If it was my own milk boy we could change dairies, but you can hardly ask a neighbour to do that. There are other solutions, of course, yet they tend to involve a chase down the street at half-past seven in the morning and I never seem to have the inclination.

My main consolation is that even Rangers supporters grow up and when this one is too old to deliver milk there is always a chance he will be replaced by a Celtic fan!

7

Away from it All

THERE will always be people who want to know where flies go in the winter. Many football fans, I find, are equally curious to know where players go in their spare time. So I'm slipping this chapter in for their benefit.

Some people are convinced that after training we all hang around coffee shops and spend hours in snooker halls. And I believe this was the case not so many years ago. In fact, I'm told in those days you could find the majority of Glasgow's football stars any day if you knew which coffee haunt or billiards room to visit. Today you could tramp round the city centre most afternoons and find few footballers.

Habits have changed, I think, because wages have increased. Players in a successful team can make quite big money now and as soon as they have enough capital they are eager to get into business for themselves. When most of the big names finish training nowadays they are too busy looking after their investments and worrying about profit and loss, etc., to think about playing snooker.

In the present Celtic side, for instance, I'm one of a minority who have no outside business interests. Jim Craig has his dental practice. Ronnie Simpson has a sports equipment shop. Willie Wallace is a partner in a garage business and John Clark has a similar part interest in a firm of decorators and Willie O'Neill has had a grocer's shop for some time. And we've got a proper 'bevy' of publicans, if that's the right phrase. At the time of writing the boys behind the bar are: Bertie Auld and Joe McBride who jointly own a public house in London Road; Billy McNeill in Bellshill; and John Hughes in Coatbridge.

Frankly, I've never thought very seriously about going into

business so far. My main objective is to keep out of doors, because fitness plays a big part in modern football and I like to move around in the fresh air as much as possible. That's why I play golf when I can and I enjoy fishing, but my No. 1 hobby is definitely shooting. A few years ago I started to go out occasionally to the open country around Clelland which was handy when I stayed at home in Motherwell, but since I became friendly with a Crieff farmer in the past two years I have jumped into the car and headed for Perthshire at every opportunity. In fact, I've now got Willie Wallace and Jimmy Johnstone almost as keen as myself, and this summer we jointly bought the shooting rights for a bit of land near Crieff.

Actually, even if I'm not shooting I spend as much time as I can on the farm, just driving a tractor or helping in any way I can. My wife Ann likes it too and I think our daughter Karen Michelle, who is a year old now, has also become quite fond of the outdoor life. With all this outdoor chat I know I must sound like 'a farmer's boy', yet there's no reason why I should because my dad, Alf, is a turner in the steelworks at Motherwell. When I left school I began work there too as an apprentice electrician. You don't get much fresh air in a steelworks and that may be why I am so keen on the outdoor life now.

I was in that job for four and a half years and would have completed my apprenticeship in another six months . . . but that was when I decided my future lay in football. I trained at Parkhead first when I was seventeen, then I signed a provisional form and went to Coltness United as an amateur. After a season in the Juniors I was invited to become a full-time professional with Celtic.

Naturally, I was bursting to say 'yes', yet it seemed like a good idea to finish my apprenticeship. So I rushed to see my boss and asked him if I could work the last six months on a part-time basis and so be able to report at Parkhead every morning. He said 'No.' In fact, I thought he was pretty unreasonable. So I went straight back and signed the full-

E

time forms and there and then said goodbye to my prospects of becoming a full-fledged electrician.

Although I still know enough about the trade to do most jobs, I must admit I have not tried very hard to 'keep my hand in'. If something breaks down at home I fix it, but I don't look for work and my electrical activity since I left the steelworks has only extended as far as putting a few plugs in for Joe McBride when he moved into a new house. Still, if the floodlights ever fail at Parkhead when we are four goals ahead—I'll be glad to look at the fuses!

Although I've mentioned Joe, Willie, and Jimmy here I must point out that, unlike many clubs, there are no cliques at Parkhead and if someone says he is having a house party the whole team are liable to turn up with their wives. Another favourite way of spending a night out is to meet somewhere for a meal and a dance. Ann and I are lucky to be able to get out fairly often, as my sister Anna (17) and my brother David (19) never let us down if we need a baby-sitter. Incidentally, to complete the Gemmell family picture there is my mother Margaret and another sister Moira (22) and they all turn out to give me a bit of support if a particular game appeals to them.

As you can see the private life of a footballer is pretty much the same as anyone else's. In winter I sometimes play badminton at a local hall in Kirkintilloch and I think that just about covers my social outings. The golf I mentioned earlier tends to be more or less confined to the games we play on West Kilbride course during Celtic's fairly frequent visits to the seaside, at Seamill.

Most people, I think are extravagant in some way and I might as well admit my two weaknesses are cars and holidays abroad. I have had seven cars in four years—and that makes me a popular guy with the salesmen. Travel agents are kind to me because I make a point of having a good holiday every year no matter where the club may tour . . . and this is another way of making sure the folding stuff never clutters up the living-room!

8

Champions Again!

BOBBY LENNOX was in terrific form in the second half of last season. He scored some great goals. Yet the one I remember most vividly was as scrappy an affair as you could imagine. In fact, you could say he was lucky the ball went in at all.

It began with a Bobby Murdoch cross from the right. As John Hughes went up for the ball there was a Morton man in front of him and another behind. 'Yogi' never really managed a header, but the ball glanced off the top of his head and that brought it out to Willie Wallace who had a quick swing and missed. Bobby Lennox, almost beside him, turned quickly and just managed to get his foot to the ball. It was hardly a shot at all and as Morton 'keeper Andy Crawford rushed out it missed his legs by a fraction of an inch. Then it sailed into the goal and over the line. The ref. was pointing to the centre of the field. It was a goal.

Yes, it was the winning goal . . . only thirty seconds before the final whistle. I've never known such a feeling of relief in my life. All I wanted to do was grab Bobby, the man who had saved our bacon. But when I ran after him I couldn't catch him because he was going too fast. He raced to the side of the pitch to the crowd. Because there were 51,000 people in Parkhead that Saturday afternoon and I think we all went a wee bit mad. I seem to remember running and jumping around on my own and when I got near the side of the pitch there was a policeman walking along the track. I got my eye on his helmet and there was an awful temptation to grab it for a bit of a carry-on. Then just at that moment I saw a police inspector standing further back. He must have been a mind-reader because as our eyes met he raised a finger and shook his head as if to say: 'No, I wouldn't do that!' So I left the

constable's helmet alone because by then I had spotted the
Boss. He was out of his dug-out, running up the touchline
shouting: 'It's time up, it's time up.' Then I joined the scrum
of players who were nearly killing wee Bobby with their
congratulations.

Now I know all this must sound like a terrible way for
grown men to be carrying on. So maybe I had better try a bit
harder to explain exactly how we felt.

That game against Morton was on April 20 this year. It
was our second from last League fixture of the season and we
had kicked off knowing we had only to win these last two
games to become Scottish champions for the third year in
succession. Which was why 50,000 had turned out to encourage us.

We never imagined, mark you, it was going to be an easy
game. Morton had done us a favour the previous Wednesday
by holding Rangers to a draw at Cappielow. The Greenock
men were still desperate for League points when they met us
because they still had a chance of qualifying for a place in
the Fairs Cities Cup.

Personally, I was convinced in the first few minutes the
game was going to be no cakewalk. I made a couple of bad
passes early on; Bobby Lennox sent one or two the wrong
way too; and when these things happen you can sense things
are not going to go your way. Even after Willie Wallace
headed the opening goal in fourteen minutes we still made
mistakes, and when Joe Mason scored from thirty yards just
before the interval I wasn't a bit surprised.

At half-time we heard that Rangers, who had been exactly
level with us on points, were also drawing with Kilmarnock.
I couldn't get the thought out of my mind that if they scored
and we didn't they would be odds-on favourites for the
championship. The longer the second half lasted the more we
pinned Morton back. They were playing with ten men in
defence and Tony Taylor standing in the centre circle. Billy
McNeill covered him and the Boss kept waving me forward.

No matter how hard we tried we couldn't get the ball in the net and with about a quarter of an hour to go John Clark, who was twelfth man, signalled to me that Rangers were leading 2-1. After that I wanted to play with my eyes shut because all I was seeing was the League Flag slipping away from us.

It seemed tragic because after the 'Old Firm' game on 2 January we had played for over three months without losing a League point. We had played so well that we built up a tremendous advantage over Rangers in goal-average and then, at last, on the Wednesday we had drawn level on points too with the same number of games played.

Yet with ten minutes to go, five minutes to go, and right up to the last minute itself it seemed all our good work in the months before would be wasted. Then came Murdoch's last cross, Lennox's final shot, and the almost unbelievable realization that we had scored. Is it any wonder we all went a little bit mad? For us, it meant relief from months of tension because from the moment wee Bobby's shot went over the line we were convinced we would win the title. In fact, we didn't win it in quite the way we expected, but before I go into that I think we should take a big step back . . . right back to the beginning of the season. Because if we take it from there I think you will find it easier to understand why winning this particular championship meant so much to us all.

In the previous season we had won everything. The big one, of course was the European Cup. But we had also collected the League Flag, the Scottish Cup, the League Cup and the Glasgow Cup. It was the greatest season any club had ever had. There was nothing more for us to win . . . except the World title. So in August when the Scottish season began again we knew we couldn't do any better. I think we had the feeling that nobody expected us to do as well again. In some ways the strain was off. We were going to enjoy the feeling of being European champions. I'm sure I was a bit careless at times because, no matter who we were playing, I had the idea

at the back of my mind that things were bound to turn out
right in the end. I'm telling you how I felt because I can only
guess at what was going through the minds of other players.

Maybe at that time, with the memory of that Lisbon
victory over Inter-Milan so sharp in our minds, we were not
really interested in playing more football. I don't know all
the reasons. But I do know there was something wrong somewhere. If any players did keep their form from the previous
season they soon lost it in the general decline.

Every game was a struggle because we knew we were not
playing as we could play. Our early matches are best forgotten. It is sufficient to say that in our first game of the
season with Rangers we owed our point purely to penalty-
taking. That was in the second qualifying game of our League
Cup section when the score was 1–1. I got our goal with a
penalty—and if Andy Penman hadn't missed when Rangers
got a penalty we would have gone home empty-handed.

I am not looking for sympathy now, but we were a pretty
harassed bunch then. We knew, for instance, we were going
to be playing in the preliminary round of the European Cup.
In the past, the European champions had quite rightly been
given a bye into the first round proper. As luck would have it,
however, some obscure team withdrew at the last minute and
we were included in the preliminary draw. Worse still, we got
a tie against Kiev of Russia who were obviously going to be
a tough nut to crack.

At our best we reckon we can beat any team, but last
August we knew we had little time to find our form. As it
turned out we had too little time. We were still a struggling
team when we met Kiev and they beat us 1–0 at Parkhead.
We improved in the second leg in Russia. We could hardly do
anything else. With nothing to lose we were able to attack to
our hearts content and in that situation we're as happy as
sandboys.

Frankly, we did enough to win that game. Bobby Lennox
scored, a Billy McNeill goal was chalked off through a

borderline decision which I thought was wrong, and big 'Yogi' was robbed. He met a ball close to the line, stopped it, and shot home. But the ref. said 'no goal' because he maintained the 'keeper had been fouled. This was ridiculous because 'Yogi' never even touched him. Either of these two 'goals' would certainly have won the tie for us.

Instead, as we hammered at the Kiev defence, they broke away a couple of minutes from time and scored the equalizer almost unchallenged. You could say we were unlucky to go out of the European Cup so quickly. Yet you could also argue that a team who played as we did in the tie at Parkhead didn't deserve to be lucky.

The defeat by Kiev probably taught us a lesson. In those days we were still up in the clouds of Lisbon to a certain extent. But in the European Cup you can't afford to rest on your laurels. When you start a new season past success doesn't mean a thing. You are probably thinking that any fool should know that. Remember, however, we were not thinking so clearly then. Looking back now, I think the Lisbon success had probably gone to our heads a little . . . and, heck, I don't feel a bit ashamed about that!

A lot of the critics did not think big-headedness was our trouble, nevertheless. They began to hint that the bubble had begun to burst for the super Celts of '67. Those who had found our clean sweep hard to bear began to suggest after Kiev that we had all the breaks the previous year and now our luck was running out we were really quite an ordinary side. They didn't say so in as many words, mark you, because they were still afraid we might win the World Championship the following month and make them look foolish.

In fact, at that time we were in the process of winning the League Cup for the third year in succession, although we certainly were not playing like World champions. The qualifying section in which we were drawn with Rangers, Aberdeen, and Dundee United proved to be a penalty-taking serial. I scored one against Aberdeen in a 3–1 win at Parkhead then missed one at Tannadice where we scraped through 1–0. The next game was against Rangers at Parkhead and, amazingly, a missed spot-kick made all the difference in the world.

There would be about a quarter of an hour to go when Rangers got the award. We were already one down and hadn't been covering ourselves in glory. It was 'curtains' for us if we went two down at that stage and everyone must have known this, including Kai Johansen as he stepped forward to take the kick.

The fact that Penman had already missed one against us may have put an extra strain on Kai because he couldn't score either. What an escape! It worked wonders on us. We suddenly began playing like a machine and by the final whistle we had scored three goals for a good-looking victory, when only a few minutes earlier you wouldn't have backed us with somebody else's money. For me, this was just another proof that you never know what will happen in an 'Old Firm' game.

In the League Cup quarter-finals we were drawn against Ayr United and although we beat the Second Division men 8–2 on a two-game aggregate this was no real guide to our form.

Our semi-final, however, was a different kettle of fish. We met Morton at Hampden and we didn't beat them, we pulverized them. They played well—and we played like European champions! We kept up a terrific pace, with everyone running off the ball exactly as they should do. We scored seven goals and the only one we lost was to a brilliant shot by their Danish wing-half Arentoft.

The Cappielow boys were unlucky to meet us that night because we had been building up to such a spree. The previous Saturday, for instance, we had a good 4–0 victory at Parkhead over Hibs who had started the season well and until then looked as if they might be serious championship challengers. The first sign that we were really beginning to get our form back had come the previous Saturday when we won 4–0 at Stirling.

A narrow escape for Hibs as Jimmy Johnstone, on the ground,
just misses a cross

Billy McNeill comes to the rescue as Ronnie Simpson is beaten by
a scoring effort from Peter Cormack of Hibs

Ronnie Simpson makes a save in the last game of the season against Dunfermline

A neat lob—and Bobby Lennox scores a goal against Dundee

It's Celtic's 100th goal of last season

Celtic *v.* Morton . . . after Willie Wallace had scored

With opponents all round, Bobby Lennox heads one of his many goals

This shows two disgusted Morton players after Bobby Lennox got our last-minute winner at Parkhead

The Albion may not be anybody's idea of stiff opposition. Nevertheless, Annfield is a ground where we often have to struggle for results, so it was a nice feeling to win that day with something in hand. The most surprising thing about that match, as far as I was concerned, was that I was in the team at all!

I had been on the injured list and although the trouble had pretty well cleared up I presumed I would still be out that weekend. The Boss gave me no indication I was playing, so at lunch-time I had a right good meal. Yessir, I did a thorough job on that menu. So it was a bit of a shaker when Neilly Mochan came out of the dressing-room less than half an hour before the kick-off and told me: 'The Boss wants you to play.' I got stripped smartly and tried not to think of all that stuff in my stomach.

And you know what? I had, what I reckoned, was my best game since the beginning of August. Suddenly my confidence seemed to come flooding back and every time I got the ball I knew exactly what I was going to do with it. It was one of those days when I wanted to 'do a Jim Baxter' and shout: 'Jist pit the ba' at ma feet!'

Had this been an ordinary season I think the end of October would have seen us in peak form and we would probably never have looked back. But the uppermost thought in our minds that month was the World Championship 'decider' with Argentina's Racing Club. We played the first leg at Hampden on the 18th then flew to South America ten days later, only hours after the League Cup Final at Hampden. I don't think the prospect of the trip affected our play against Dundee that day. We were determined to have a Cup at our back before we left home and we won 5–3 despite mistakes in defence.

We didn't know then that the South American trip was going to shatter the confidence which we had taken so long to regain. Maybe that sounds as if I am sorry for myself. Well, I don't want anyone to get out their hankie and cry. But I don't think some people realize how badly our team was affected by these games against Racing Club.

Our record last season was pretty sensational when you consider what a setback we suffered in those early days of November. Okay, so we lost and I know every team has to be able to get over a disappointment. We had also to get over our anger (which I've explained in another chapter), illness, and injury. Jim Craig, for instance, caught a virus over there which left him with a badly upset stomach for weeks. And the rest of us found it blooming difficult to come back and go on playing as if nothing had happened.

The Press made it virtually impossible. Some writers seemed determined to prove that any kicking we did in the last twenty minutes of the third game against Racing was ten times worse than all the crimes they committed in the 250 minutes before then. There was hardly a week in which we didn't pick up a paper and find some critic asking when the S.F.A. were going to do something about our behaviour in South America, especially against the players who were ordered off. Does anyone really believe this didn't affect Celtic's form at the end of last year? Any time the boys got together it was a fair bet 'suspensions' would become the topic of conversation, and some of the lads worried about it. There was more than one occasion when I heard someone ask: 'Could they put us out for a couple of months?' We had read so much about it for so long we began to feel as if we had committed a murder instead of a justifiable bit of football retaliation.

Yet when we came back from Montevideo we still managed to keep on winning our League games although, goodness knows, they weren't victories you would want to write home about. I remember, for instance, the game against Raith Rovers at Starks Park.

In those days Raith were everybody's idea of a 'sure thing' for relegation and this was the kind of fixture which the supporters are inclined to treat as a foregone conclusion. Yet

Raith are a team who were determined to keep playing football and as we now know it eventually got them away from the foot of the table. That day they were a tricky bunch too and at half-time there was no scoring. In the end we won 2–0 and by that time I had scored with a penalty . . . and missed one. In that period we always seemed to have a feeling of relief rather than triumph when we heard the final whistle.

At least we left Starks Park with the points, which was more than we could do the following week at home to Dundee United. If you look back on our entire League programme you can see quite clearly there was a lesson to be learned that day.

That was the day an injury forced the Boss to pull Willie Wallace back to right-half. This meant he was in direct opposition to the left-winger Davie Wilson who played many a game against us for Rangers. This pair didn't get on at all and a little private war ended with 'Wispy' being sent off after a clash with the blond Davie. We lost more than a player, however. We lost a point, because the game ended 1–1.

The interesting thing is that the only other time we had dropped a point at home was back in September on the day when wee Jimmy Johnstone was sent off after an incident with St. Johnstone winger Kenny Aird. The score was 1–1 then too.

Two men ordered off . . . two points lost. I'm not the preaching type and I've been known to lose the head very occasionally myself, but it makes our chairman Bob Kelly's argument look pretty strong. He has always insisted that discipline must come before success. Through the years he has made it clear he does not want to see a Celtic player in trouble with the referee. And in these two games you must admit he got a lot of backing for his case.

If we had not lost these two points at home we would have been under much less strain in the rest of our League programme. As it was we struggled up to the end of the year with a 3–2 home win over Dunfermline and a scramble home by the same score at Shawfield on New Year's Day.

Then on the following day we met Rangers at Parkhead. This was the game that mattered. They had already beaten us 1–0 at Ibrox early in the season and another win would have made them red-hot favourites for the Flag. The newspapers called this game 'a championship decider' . . . which sounds pretty silly when you think of the desperate battles both clubs had to fight for points towards the end of the season. I don't blame the papers, of course, they must try to make games dramatic and most of the supporters looked upon this as a 'decider' anyway.

Frankly, we were convinced we could win. Although Rangers were still undefeated and by then under a new manager, their performances weren't exactly scintillating and we reckoned we must be better than they even if we were not at our best. But as I've said before and will say again later— YOU CAN BE SURE OF NOTHING IN AN 'OLD FIRM' MATCH!

We played well. In fact, for most of the game we were a mile ahead in everything, except the art of finishing. In the event we scored two goals and I think anyone would agree we did more than enough to win that game. Yet we had to settle for a 2–2 draw.

Ronnie Simpson had been injured the previous day against Clyde and so John Fallon was in goal in the 'Old Firm' game. John has had some terrific games for us, but this wasn't one of them. I think every player in his career has a game he wants to forget completely. We were going well and shaping as if we were going to have a really good win when Willie Johnston shot and John let the ball go through his legs into the net. It was a heartbreaking goal to lose in such a vital match and it put new life into Rangers. Nevertheless, we managed to get a grip of the game again and in the closing minutes we led 2–1 and were set for a win which nobody could have grudged us.

But suddenly, with about a minute to go, there was Kai Johansen bursting into our penalty area and having a shot.

He didn't get it 'on' properly, however, there was little power behind it, and John Fallon was in good position. Yet amazingly, unbelievably, he seemed to dive after the ball had passed him. One blunder in a game like that was bad enough, but two was ridiculous!

In the dressing-room, where everyone was disgusted, John seemed to come through his ordeal well. He had a quick bath and managed to whistle as he combed his hair. I remember it annoyed me to see him looking so cheery after such a disaster. Later I realized he must simply have been putting on a brave front until he got away on his own.

Poor John didn't get much sympathy that day and it must have been a pretty miserable New Year for him. But after we got over the disappointment of losing two points when they had been there for the taking, I think we were all the more determined than ever to win the League for Fallon's sake. Because we knew, as he did, that if we lost it he would be remembered as the man who had cost us the championship—and the blokes on the terracing would make sure he didn't forget it.

As they say in the racing papers, we were 'carrying top weight' from that game onwards. We had lost our chance to close the points gap with Rangers so we knew our only chance of the championship was to go on winning and hope they made mistakes. It was quite a strain to go into the second half of the League programme knowing we had used up our quota of mistakes and couldn't afford even another one.

So we kept on winning, home and away. We beat Hibs, Partick Thistle, and Motherwell. Our Motherwell victory was a 1–0 affair, yet indirectly it did us a lot of good. We still hadn't produced anything like our best form and that day the Boss must have decided it was time for drastic action.

On the following Tuesday morning he called us all into the table-tennis room at Parkhead where we hold many of our big debates. I don't remember his exact words, but he told us bluntly that while we might be winning we were not playing anything like as well as we could. So it was high time we did something about it. If there was anything we wanted changed; anything bothering us at all; he wanted to know. He even offered to change the training routine if we weren't happy about it.

In fact, it was during that discussion he came up with an idea which would have made us different from any team in Britain. He said if we wanted a bit of variety we could alternate with the reserves. We could train in the mornings one week then train in the afternoons the next. It was decided, however, to postpone that move for a week or so until we found whether we could get back on the rails or not. Some people, I bet, will be thinking we would have been better out on the field instead of sitting talking, but they couldn't be more wrong. The two hours we spent in that table-tennis room had a lot to do with us winning the League!

That morning, after all, we had to find answers. We had to work out why we were not playing as well as we should have been. And I think we succeeded. You see, as the talk went on everybody got the chance to say his piece. We talked about the game in general. We argued about little things that had happened in recent matches. Until gradually we realized that we were no longer using some of the good moves which had paid off for us the previous season.

Later in the week we got out on to the field and practised these moves, especially those which were designed to bring goals. For one of the things we all agreed on in our conflab was that we had to boost the scoring rate in League matches. Rangers still had to drop a couple of points before we had any chance of the title, but if they did, then goal average would count. And that was something we reckoned we could skin them on, as we have more potential scorers than they.

Besides that, we reckoned it was our duty to give the fans goals even if we couldn't give them the championship.

As they say in Whitehall, the debate continued, and

gradually we got to talking about the future. The Boss asked us what we would like to see the club doing, and we soon told him. A chorus of voices pleaded with him to fix matches as often as he could with the world's top teams. These are the games we really enjoy. We know we can beat anyone, and when the opposition puts on a bit of a show this brings the best out in us.

In the past couple of years we have cuffed Manchester United, Real Madrid, Inter-Milan, and Penarol. 'These are the teams we want to play,' we told the Boss. And having played and won at that level I might as well admit it can be difficult to work up enthusiasm sometimes for matches against the poorer Scottish teams.

Nevertheless, our next game was against Stirling Albion and the two points at stake were just as vital as any others in our drawn-out battle with Rangers. We beat Albion 2-0 in one of those games which are not easily remembered . . . yet it was important in a way.

For that was the beginning of a six-match League run in which we scored 24 goals and lost 1. Yessir, that's the stuff big healthy goal-averages are made of—and in that spell I'm sure we put a greater strain on the Light Blues, because they weren't winning anything like as easily.

The biggest and best of these victories was against Kilmarnock at Rugby Park a week after the Scotland–England game at Hampden. We really won because wee Jimmy Johnstone was fantastic. The wee man was probably just proving he shouldn't have been left out of the Scottish team.

Mark you, I'm not pretending I worried very much about his reasons. When you see somebody in your team playing like that all you want to do is applaud. Jimmy wasn't just playing for the bonus money that day, he seemed to be all out for a Nobel Prize! Honestly, he roasted those Killie defenders as if he had a grudge against them all his life. And since that kind of thing is catching, the only surprising thing is that we scored just six goals.

That was the day we really got through to the sports writers. They all agreed we had got back to our best form at last. They wrote later that our revival began at Rugby Park. They didn't know some of the things they saw stemmed from a two-hour talk in the table-tennis room at Parkhead.

I've a feeling, however, we didn't get too much credit, because at this time everybody was talking about Rangers. For about that time they made what I thought was one of the worst decisions in their history. They were due to meet us in the semi-final of the Glasgow Cup . . . but instead of playing they withdrew. They said they had too many fixtures because they were due to play Hearts in the Scottish Cup and Leeds in the Fairs Cities Cup. This sounded a pretty lame excuse, considering we had overcome the same kind of problem the previous season and still managed to win everything. It was certainly an annoying decision as far as we players were concerned. The Rangers boys were upset because they had been denied the chance to prove themselves against us. We were annoyed because we had been foiled at a time when we were convinced we would have outclassed them. The public had no doubts. They reckoned Rangers' bosses were afraid their team would get a hiding.

But I honestly think Rangers made a big mistake here for the reasons I've mentioned earlier. There is no such thing as a 'foregone conclusion' when we meet the Light Blues. No matter how confident we may have been, there is nothing to say we would have won. Results throughout the years prove this. But the Ibrox officials did not have to look that far back. In this same season they had watched Penman miss a penalty; Johansen miss a penalty; and Fallon having his nightmare. Surely the message was clear. You should never 'chicken out' of an 'Old Firm' game because anything can happen . . . and anybody can win!

So while Rangers were backing out of the Glasgow Cup; blundering out of the Scottish Cup; and not even getting a goal against Leeds in the Fairs Cup; we were bowling merrily along. We took four goals from Aberdeen, four from Airdrie, three from Falkirk, and five from Raith Rovers.

Then we went to Perth and beat St. Johnstone 6–1. But there were no medals going from the Boss for that performance. He was on the warpath over the goal we lost.

Saints, you see, had scored from a free-kick. It should never have happened if we had all covered a man properly. So when the Boss got us together for training the following week he took us out to the practice pitch at Barrowfield and we worked out how we were going to deal with this kind of free-kick. And when I say we worked I'm not kidding. For two hours solid we did nothing but clear free-kicks away from the goal-mouth. All I hope is the St. Johnstone boys didn't have half as much trouble with the six we scored as we had with their little effort.

I thought I would tell you this story because it helps to show what top professional football is all about. In schools football and even higher grades one free-kick is much the same as another and everyone crowds back and tries to scramble the ball away somewhere. There's much more planning going on at a free-kick during a professional match than spectators realize. Every defender has a job to do and the arrangements may vary according to where the kick is coming from. Teams like Leeds United who are prepared to defend for much of a game can only do this because they have left very little to chance.

We lost no goals in our next League game, partly because we were rarely under pressure and also because Ronnie Simpson made a couple of great saves. This was the match with Dundee United at Tannadice where we won 5–0 and Jimmy Johnstone got all the headlines again.

No wonder! Only he could have scored the opening goal. He beat two men then shot past the 'keeper and I reckon the whole operation was carried out in the space of about seven feet. He had a hand in most of the other goals that day too.

F

In fact, if the wee man doesn't mind me saying so, I think that was maybe the day he grew up as a player.

By that I mean I had never seen him read a game so well before. Jimmy, in my book, has always been a world-beater. The trouble was he often wanted to beat the world in the one run! The first signs of the change, I think, were in the game at Kilmarnock and in the weeks that followed he stuck up some shrewd passes. But at Tannadice he was brilliant. He would hold the ball until he spotted someone in a good position then give them a great ball. He was even spreading it with the side of his foot like De Stefano. In other seasons you could shout at him until you were blue in the face, but he wouldn't let the ball go until he had nobody left to beat. Now he was actually looking for the moment when a pass would do most good. I don't know how he felt, but it did me a lot of good that day just watching him.

I felt even better a few days later. That was when Rangers went to Tannadice and on the ground where we had won so comfortably they dropped a point. By then we had established a much superior goal average to John Greig and his chums. So with a handful of games to play there was really only a point between us and the title. Rangers, of course, had to drop that point and we had to go on winning. Yet we were pretty optimistic because at that stage we had played eleven games in a row without dropping a point, and with the loss of only three goals!

I'm not pretending we weren't under a strain, just as Rangers were. No game is easy when you go out knowing you MUST win. Nevertheless, in our next Saturday game we took two more points from Hearts at Tynecastle and on the following Wednesday we were due at Pittodrie.

No team ever goes to Aberdeen expecting a walk-over. Yet in the form book we were hot favourites. We had already beaten the Dons three times in the season and our League Cup visit to Pittodrie had ended in a 5–1 win. Aberdeen, of course, had made a disappointing start to the season. After doing well in the States during the summer they were expected to make a real show last season, but instead they took a long, long time to get going.

I think they must have been waiting for our League game in April. That night they were terrific; a good side by any standards. They certainly put up a tremendous fight and although we won 1–0 thanks to a Bobby Lennox goal all the boys were agreed it had been our hardest League game of the season. In fact, after the game the Boss said: 'We must win the League now.'

But no matter who won the championship everybody could see it was going to be a terrific finish and hundreds of 'Old Firm' fans spent their Saturdays watching a game holding a transistor radio to their ear so they could hear how the 'other half' were doing at the same time. As we beat Dundee 5–2 at Parkhead, for instance, Raith Rovers were putting up a great fight before Rangers substitute Andy Penman scored the winning goal at Starks Park. After that game with Dundee we had another 'post mortem' because George McLean had scored from the same kind of free-kick which cost us a goal against St. Johnstone.

The following Wednesday we played Clyde in the Glasgow Cup Final at Hampden. Rangers played Morton at Cappielow. And John Fallon was playing in goal in a reserve match at Parkhead. It turned out to be a great night for Celtic, but I won't tell you why because it sounds better the way John tells it:

'I don't know if I saved any shots that night, but if I did it must have been from memory. Because I played that game with my mind twenty miles away. All that interested me was the score at Cappielow and they were giving it on the loud-speakers every ten minutes. I had prayed for months that Rangers would slip up and we would win the League. I reckoned that was the only way people might forget my boobs in the New Year game.

'And that night I was sure the Morton–Rangers game

would seal my fate. If Rangers won I couldn't see them slipping up in their last two games. But I was sure Celtic would win the League if Morton got a point, because we would be ahead on goal average then. So when I went into goal against Raith Rovers that night I was really out there waiting for the loudspeaker announcements. Then we heard Morton were one up, then two up . . . nobody at Parkhead shouted louder than me when that news came through. Imagine Morton winning . . . I could hardly bear to think about it. That would leave us a point ahead of Rangers with two games to go. The news from Hampden was great too. The boys were scoring like a machine against Clyde. At half-time the scores were Celtic 7, Clyde 0; Morton 2, Rangers 0, and I could hardly keep a stupid grin off my face.

'But, boy, did I sweat it out in the second half. First we heard Rangers had scored. Then it was 3–1 for Morton; 3–2 for Morton. And when they said it was 3–3 at Cappielow I didn't want to hear any more announcements. I knew that if Rangers got another goal and won after being two down there would be no holding them—and I would be the guy who had thrown the championship at Parkhead! I didn't know whether to stand still or walk about. I didn't even know how many minutes were left for play. But finally the final whistle went. I gathered we had beaten Raith 2–1, although if they had beaten us 10–0 I probably wouldn't have noticed. The final scores, of course, were Morton 3, Rangers 3; Celtic 8, Clyde 0. Aye, a great night for Celtic . . . But I never want to spend ninety minutes like that again!'

You see what I mean? It must have been murder for John, but the fact is the Cappielow game affected every Celtic player that night. It certainly had a bearing on the score in our final at Hampden. We had been going forward from the first kick of the ball and it was one of those nights everybody was in the mood. Apart from scoring goals we were making plenty of chances and I remember a great 25-yarder by Bobby Lennox which rattled the crossbar.

It seemed to me we were scoring every time we went up the field. According to the Press boys, however, our tally was seven goals in thirty-five minutes. We were in pretty good spirits therefore when Queen's Park coach Harold Davis came into the dressing-room at half-time and said: 'Morton are beating Rangers 2–0.' We didn't believe him at first. Harry, after all, is an ex-Rangers man and we were sure he was just saying that for a bit of mischief. Then we realized he meant it. What a feeling!

I remember going out for the start of the second half against Clyde . . . but I'm sure my feet never touched the ground. One thing that shook me that night was how quick news can spread in a crowd. As I went on to the track I saw three of our supporters at the side of the tunnel. This bloke and his two girl friends always seem to manage to get a place near the tunnel no matter where we are playing. As I passed I told them the score at Cappielow—and the effect was amazing. In a matter of seconds the word seemed to spread to hundreds of fans and I could hear a roar starting to build up.

The sports writers said we slackened off after the interval against Clyde, because we got only one more goal from Bobby Murdoch. It must have looked as if we didn't want to be hard on the Shawfield boys. We had already equalled the record score for a Glasgow Cup Final. In fact, by that time we were all like John Fallon. We could hardly keep our minds on the Hampden game for thinking about what was happening at Cappielow. John Clark, who was twelfth man again, was working overtime in the dug-out as a tic-tac man keeping us up to date with the score.

Well, as you know, Rangers dropped a point and we won a Cup, but I don't want to leave that night without mentioning the Clyde team. They were unlucky to meet us when we were in top gear, yet two of their players still stood out. Right-half Stan Anderson got through a terrific amount of work and I'm inclined to think Stan is one of the most under-rated players in Scottish football. As far as I can see he doesn't have many bad games and I might say the same for Harry Hood. Harry did not get much scope at Hampden as Clyde were pinned back most of the time, yet he hit the post when the score was 1–0 and if that one had gone in it might have been a different match.

The following Saturday Rangers had to play Kilmarnock at Rugby Park and we were at home to Morton . . . which brings me back to where I began this story of our 1967–8 League championship win. You can see now why I died a thousand deaths before Bobby Lennox got his last-minute winner against Morton.

By then we were so near to the title it would have been a heartbreak to lose it. As it was, both halves of the 'Old Firm' won 2–1 that day. This left Rangers and ourselves level on points with one game to play. We had the advantage of a better goal average, but Rangers' last game was at home while ours was away. Some people tend to knock Scottish football, but I don't think anyone could complain about a championship which had a climax like that.

As things turned out the remaining two games could hardly have been more dramatic and I think they proved there is nothing predictable about football, either on or off the field. Rangers' last fixture, for instance, was against Aberdeen at Ibrox on Saturday, April 27, Scottish Cup Final day. John Greig & Co. knew that if they beat the Dons then the strain would be on us again, knowing we had to take two points from Dunfermline at East End Park the following Tuesday. This was one of the reasons why, although we were spending a few days at Seamill the Boss brought us all back to Glasgow for the Cup Final. He wanted us to have the chance of study-ing Dunfermline when they were going all out. He also thought we should support the Final, and because many of our supporters turned out too there was a respectable attendance of 53,000, although the critics had predicted it would hit a record low as two teams from the East were taking part.

After a poor first half Dunfermline turned on the power and were far too good for Hearts. Yet for us the real excitement came after the game. We were in the car park, preparing to go back to Seamill, when the Boss ran from the main entrance at Hampden and through the crowd to tell us Aberdeen had beaten Rangers 3–2. Then we knew we were Scottish Champions again. We had won the title for the third year running. We were back in the European Cup. But we could hardly have been more surprised. It seemed fantastic that Rangers, unbeaten throughout the whole of the League programme, should allow themselves to slip up on the last day.

The Boss joined us at Seamill later that evening and he soon made it clear our last game against Dunfermline was going to be no friendly, even if we didn't need the points quite as desperately as we might have done. He told us: 'We don't want to win a title on goal average if we can win it by a couple of points. That way there can be no arguments.' In fact, next day the papers were pointing out that if we won at Dunfermline our total of 63 points would be a post-war record. We were very confident. We knew we had a good record at East End Park. We also reckoned manager George Farm's boys would find it difficult to get back to earth so soon after the emotional business of winning the Scottish Cup.

But as our bus headed through Fife that Tuesday evening on the way to East End Park we realized there was something we had not taken into consideration . . . OUR SUPPORT! You don't have to be at Parkhead very long before you realize what a fantastic bunch our supporters are, but now and again they turn out in a way which takes you by surprise. I'll never forget the time when we walked out to inspect the pitch at Lisbon before last year's European Cup Final. We were something like 1,200 miles from home, yet when we looked round the stadium all we could see was green and white flags, scarves, hats, and banners. It was just like Parkhead . . . only with sunshine!

The Dunfermline game wasn't anything like as special an

occasion. It was an end-of-season fixture, after all, and everybody knew the championship was ours. It was also a midweek evening and so most blokes didn't have much time to get to the ground after leaving work. Yet the traffic on the road was fantastic. Normally we travel to East End Park the orthodox way over Kincardine Bridge, but that night the Boss told the driver to go via the Forth road bridge. Even then we ran into a crawling queue of dozens of supporters' buses. When the police spotted us they laid on an escort and we travelled the last few miles on the wrong side of the road with the sirens screaming. Believe me, nothing starts the old butterflies in the tummy more than arriving at a ground to the sound of those police sirens. Suddenly everything seems mighty important. It's the kind of thing you associate with Cup Finals and Internationals. Cup Winners *v.* League Champions. ... It was an attractive game, yet it was our supporters who made it a really big occasion. By the time we reached the dressing-room I think we were all pretty keyed up ... and I was feeling grateful to George Farm who had given me two complimentary tickets for the stand.

It happened like this. When I got to the ground I met my mother and father. My farmer pal from Crieff, John Thom, (whom I've mentioned in another chapter), was also there with four friends. Another good friend of mine who helps me with jobs around the house was also looking for a ticket. So I had to find eight tickets. Since the players were getting four each I soon managed to get my hands on half a dozen. That left me two short. So I asked Dunfermline boss Farm if he could sell me two more. Sure enough, he produced two stand tickets, but as I offered him the money he just smiled, stamped 'Complimentary' on them, and handed them over. I thought it was a great gesture considering I was in the opposition camp.

The atmosphere in East End Park that night was something you don't easily forget. We walked out alongside Dunfermline and we both got a tremendous reception. In fact, when the Fifers did a lap of honour with the Scottish Cup the Celtic fans clapped as hard as the home crowd. The ground was packed, but unfortunately there were still a lot of people outside trying to get in. Many of them forced their way in and it was a bit of a shaker to look up and see hundreds of them on the roof of the enclosure.

Not that I had much time to look up. We started at a cracking pace and soon had Dunfermline 'on the ropes'. In fact, in the first few minutes yours truly thought he had scored a wonder goal. I got a fast ball down the left wing and when I was only a few yards from the by-line I hit it across as hard as I could. I was falling, but as I landed on the deck I saw the net bulging. From where I sat it looked a corker of a goal. Instead, referee 'Tiny' Wharton gave a free-kick and I was told later Willie Wallace had swept the ball into the net with his hand.

We had only been playing eight minutes, however, when the game was stopped. The police told the crowd on top of the enclosure that there would be no more play until they came down. I believe everybody was relieved about that, because if the roof had given way there could have been a major disaster. As far as the football was concerned the break gave Dunfermline a vital 'breather' and when we came back out we found it difficult to get going again as well as before. Pretty soon we had to go into the pavilion again when a crush barrier collapsed and the fans burst on to the field. By then there were more than 30,000 in the ground and later we found out thousands more were still outside. According to most calculations there must have been close on 35,000 Celtic fans in Dunfermline for a midweek game played nearly fifty miles from Glasgow—and I think that's a pretty fantastic kind of support which few clubs in the world could equal.

As things turned out we needed all the encouragement they could give us against the Fifers. At half-time, for instance, we were one down. Home centre Pat Gardner had burst through and scored a brilliant goal from 18 yards. By the interval, incidentally, the police, who did a great job, had the crowd completely under control with many sitting around the track. Early in the second half Bobby Lennox equalized from close in and then, with the fans making a deafening noise, we went after the winner every way we knew. With just under twenty minutes to go we got that vital goal, which made the perfect ending to the season and I don't expect anyone was surprised that the scorer was wee Bobby Lennox!

He had been scoring match-winning goals for weeks and even months so it was appropriate he should get this one.

And that just about brings me to the end of the story. We had done what we set out to do in Dunfermline that night and our fantastic supporters had made it a night to remember. I'm not forgetting the other team either. Everyone told me afterwards it was a pretty good match to watch and that says as much for Dunfermline as it does for us. They will be one of the teams we will have to treat with respect in season 1968-9 and in the years to come too, I imagine, because they are a really go-ahead club.

Their players will have more confidence after winning the Cup and they could do well in the Cup Winners' Cup. I like Pat Gardner. He's strong, takes up good position, and can hit the ball hard. Their skipper Roy Barry is a terrific player too and I would rate him Scotland's best centre-half outside of the 'Old Firm'. Hugh Robertson, who plays behind the front line, doesn't always get the credit he deserves.

What about Celtic? Well, since I haven't missed a League game in the three seasons we have won the championship I've been in a good position to see what everybody else was doing. Basically we win games because we all work at it; we keep running; and in the end the pace we set is too much for a lot of teams. We have also had a great half-back line in Murdoch, McNeill, and Clark. This is essential in any good side and when it was broken up through an injury to John Clark near the end of last season Jim Brogan fitted in amazingly well, and if Willie O'Neill and Charlie Gallagher aren't always in the team they never let us down when called upon. I've already said my piece about Jimmy Johnstone and that goes for Jim Craig too. Although Willie Wallace is a regular in attack his ability to play anywhere has proved invaluable on more than one occasion. John Hughes is the kind of guy whose exploits speak for themselves. Nobody knows what will happen when 'Yogi' is around, but, boy, he scores some cracking goals. In our 8-0 win over Clyde in the Glasgow Cup, for instance, he hit the ball on the turn from 20 yards and Tommy McCulloch never knew a thing about it until it was in the net.

There's been plenty written about Ronnie Simpson already. He's an amazing man for his age is 'faither'. But he's still a good 'keeper and I can think of a lot of games we won last year only after the auld yin had made a vital save when the game was level or we were maybe just one up. These are the saves which 'sicken' the opposition.

Anyone who saw our League game at Pittodrie when we scraped home by a solitary goal will remember how much we owed to this amazing bloke who was playing senior for Queen's Park when I was in nappies!

Supporters' clubs, as you have probably noticed, are fond of picking a 'Player of the Year'. Their choice varies so much that dozens of players from various clubs can expect to get an honour at the end of every season. But if I look back on last season, which has naturally been clearest in my mind as I write this book, I can see Celtic's 'Player of the Year' sticking out a mile. He's a wee bloke—and he's got the kind of legs which make you think he should have a wee horse as well! He's a cheery character who can move after a ball like greased lightning. He was Scotland's leading scorer last season and at his best is as big a menace to goalkeepers as anybody in Britain.

Yes, of course, I mean Bobby Lennox. In the past he had a habit of playing about a dozen good games then losing form for a while. But not last season. With Willie Wallace switching positions and losing a bit of form like everyone else at times, Lennox was left to carry the can in front himself in most games. He didn't let us down. I've already mentioned a lot of the vital goals he scored for us, but I also believe that by the end of the season he was also reading the game better than ever before. I wouldn't try to pick out his best goal because they all looked good to me. His greatest performance was probably the Glasgow Cup Final. He grabbed a hat-trick against Clyde that night; made the pass for one or two more; and had bad luck with lots of others. In that kind of form you feel everything Bobby touches will turn to goals!

I only hope he keeps it up for a long time to come . . .

9

Another European Cup

THEY say only a fool makes predictions in football. Well, that may be true. But with all my good looks nobody expects me to be clever too! So I'll make a prediction now. I'll say that, provided we get no serious injuries, Celtic will win the European Cup for a second time in 1969.

I realize we may have played our first-round tie by the time you read this book, but I don't think my forecast is the least bit rash. It's really just a question of logic. We won the European Cup in 1967 because we were the best side in the competition. We proved to everyone, including Inter-Milan, that attack is still the best means of defence. And I expect us to win the Cup again because we are more effective in attack than any of the rest.

But I should explain that this opinion is not mine alone. Last April, when our League Championship battle with Rangers was drawing to a climax, most of our first team travelled to Manchester to watch United beat Real Madrid 1–0 at Old Trafford in the semi-final of the European Cup.

Real were content to defend and United, even with George Best, Bobby Charlton, and Denis Law in their team, were able to do little about it. In fact, in the end their attack depended to a great extent on crosses into the goalmouth by wing-half Paddy Crerand.

We were all in great spirits after the game because what we saw convinced us we could beat either of these teams, and the fact that they had reached the semi-finals showed how far we would have gone again if Kiev hadn't caught us on the hop at the beginning of the season before we had found our feet. That was our own fault, of course, but we won't make that kind of mistake again. We learned a lot from that Old

Trafford game, incidentally. We saw how much United depend on Best in attack, for instance. You can't blame them for that, of course. George is a great player. I know that to my cost. He gave me a roasting in our international against Ireland in Belfast last season and I would never envy anyone who has to play against him. You see, he has this amazing knack of never losing control of the ball. As you wait to tackle him there are moments when he seems to have let the ball run too far ahead. That's when you go in. But the ball isn't there because somehow he has managed to get a foot to it and you are well beaten. You can't make any plans to force him down one side either because he has the ball control to beat his man either way.

Another thing I admire about Best is his courage. He hasn't a great physique by any means, yet you will never see him shirking the tackle. But the interesting thing about that game at Old Trafford was the way in which Best was eventually subdued by Real's left-back Sanchis. He is a good player, yet when we played Real in Madrid the week after our European Cup win Jimmy Johnstone gave this boy a roasting. Another player who impressed me in the game with United was Real right-half Pirri. This bloke was brilliant in defence and he showed he could come through with the ball too. Unlike most Latin players he will take a bit of punishment and still come back hard himself.

United were lucky that night Amancio didn't play. He is Real's best forward and he would have given United trouble even working on his own. As it was, the Real attack did not show much. The great Gento's best days are now over. I realized this the previous year in Madrid, when he was barracked repeatedly by the Spanish fans.

If Real fall below our standards in attack United are equally under par in defence. They badly lack pace in this department and I think Jimmy Johnstone could have a field-day against their left flank. Actually, as United, Leeds, and Manchester City fought out a battle for the English title last season we didn't really care which one of them might join us in the European Cup. After all, we were the first British side to reach the Final of the European Cup, let alone win it, so why should we fear any team south of the border?

In the European Cup, of course, you must treat every opponent with respect, as they are their country's champions. At the same time it is obvious that the football standards in more than half the countries taking part are well below ours in Scotland. There are probably twenty teams, therefore, whom you know you can beat unless you make stupid mistakes and play well below form.

Basically, only a handful of teams in the competition are potential champions, but the standards set by this group are naturally very high. Although I would include A.C. Milan in this group because they are the former champions I cannot see them as a threat to us since, being Italians, their strength is sure to lie in a tight defence. I think our style of play will always overcome this kind of team.

My guess is that the most formidable team in the competition this season will turn out to be Hungary's Ferencvaros. Like the Scots, the Hungarian sides usually have several players with a lot of natural ability and their teamwork is always well developed. With Ferencvaros, of course, their form in last season's Fairs Cities Cup speaks for itself.

Long before the draw was made we all agreed there were two teams we wanted to meet in this season's European Cup —Kiev and Real Madrid!

I'm sure our reasons for wanting Kiev are all too obvious. We were just hankering for a bit of revenge. I think Madrid are the team everyone wants to meet. Not just because of their record in the Cup, but because they are a really sporting side and you know they will allow you to play football.

One of the snags about British teams meeting in these European competitions is that the games are spoiled by too much feeling. If we are playing an English side, for instance it becomes Scotland *v.* England all over again and as often

as not there is too much physical contact. This is silly when
you think of it, because European prestige should matter a lot
more than the kind we and the English get from beating each
other.

Anyway, as I've said, I am sure we can win this Cup again.
Nobody wins anything, however, unless they've got something to drive them on and bring out that little extra effort.
In 1967 our spur was that no British side had reached the
Final before. Now I think our incentive is the desire to redeem
ourselves. We know we flopped in the first round last season
and in the eyes of everyone we failed in the World Championship 'decider', no matter the reason. So if we win in Europe
again that will put the record right. Nobody, not even the
English sports writers, will be foolish enough to say then that
our first success was a fluke.

I think the football public will want us to win too. Because
we try to give them value for money, by sticking the ball in
the net as often as possible. If we don't make a hit in the
European Cup again, then it might be won by one of those
miserable teams whose only aim in life is not to lose a goal.
That would be terrible.

Real Madrid built their fabulous reputation in the European Cup with a great forward line which scored a pile of
goals. We want to do the same. In fact, I can't believe there is
any player who doesn't get a kick out of seeing the ball going
into the net. I know that as far as Mrs. Gemmell's big son
Tommy is concerned there is no greater feeling than running
up and having a dirty great bash at the ball.

And if it finishes in the bag? YAHOO! Boy, that's LIVING!